STEAM and RAIL in
SLOVAKIA

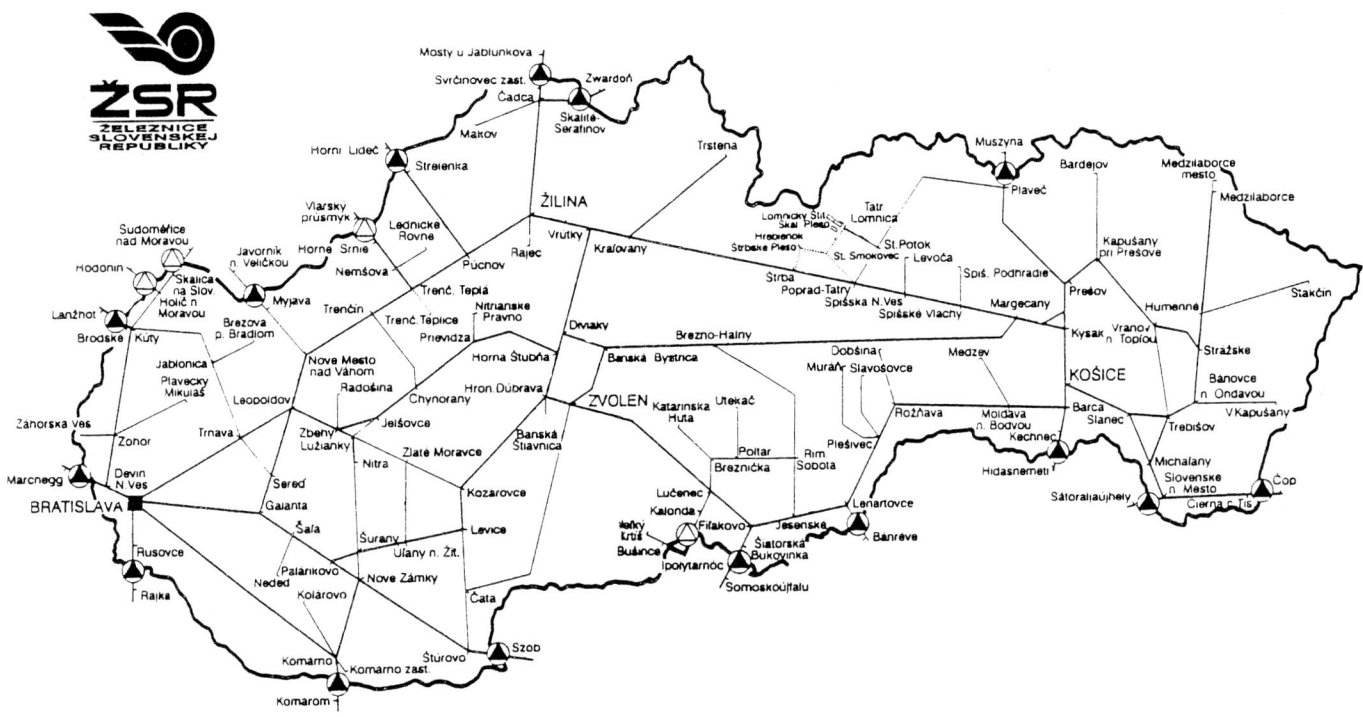

Paul Catchpole

A Locomotives International Publication

STEAM & RAIL IN SLOVAKIA

FRONT COVER:
The magnificent express passenger 'Albatross' class 4-8-2 no. 498.104, restored to operating condition and on display at Hlohovec on 4th October 1997. This locomotive was designed to work heavy trains at 120 kph and match the timings for electric traction.
Photo: Paul Catchpole.

REAR COVER:
755.001-5 is a reconstructed and thoroughly modernised 'Goggles' class Bo-Bo, with an appearance just as imposing. Designers Martinská Mechatronická are using this loco as the pilot project for a widespread modernisation of the ŽSR diesel fleet, the concept of which is to apply the latest technology, but re-using as much of the original loco as possible.   Photo: Martinská Mechatronická a.s.

FRONTISPIECE:
Although built for top link express work, the 486.0 class were also suitable for freight. 486.004, with double Kylchap exhaust heads a goods through Horný Hričov on the Váh Valley route west of Žilina, on 19th August 1958.   Photo: A.E. Durrant.

British Library Cataloguing in Publication Data. A catalogue record for this book is available from the British Library.

© 1998 *Locomotives International* and authors.
All rights reserved. No part of this book may be reproduced or transmitted in any form or by any means without prior written permission from the publisher.

ISBN 1-900340-08-9
First Edition. Published by Paul Catchpole Ltd., Kings Norton, Birmingham, England
Printed and bound by Neografia, Martin, Slovakia

STEAM AND RAIL IN SLOVAKIA

Contents

Introduction - Slovakia: A Land of Rivers, Mountains, Forests and Railways	4
The First Railways in Slovakia	7
The Váh Valley Railway	10
The Tisza District Railway	13
The ÁVT - Austro-Hungarian State Railway Co.	15
The Hungarian North Eastern Railway	17
The First Hungarian - Galician Railway	18
Magyar Államvasút - MÁV	19
The Košice - Bohumín Railway	27
Motive power on the KBD (steam)	33
Electric traction on the KBD	37
Railways in the Tatras	
The Poprad Valley Railway	39
The Štrba - Štrbské Pleso Railway*	39
The Tatra Electric Railway*	41
Czechoslovakian State Railways	43
ČSD Narrow Gauge Lines	
Ružomberok - Korytnice	49
Trenčiankska Teplá - Trenčianske Teplice*	52
Užhorod - Antalovce*	53
Narrow Gauge Forestry Railways	
Kysuce - Orava Forestry Railway	54
Povážská Lesná Železnica, Liptovský Hrádok*	55
Hronec Forestry Railway	56
Former Metre Gauge Railways	
Hronská Dúbrava - Banská Štiavnica	57
Margecany - Gelnica - Smolník*	62
Armoured Trains in Slovakia	63
Working on the Railways	68

Acknowledgements:
With special thanks for assistance in preparation of this edition: to Alena Forest for the introduction, ing. Juraj Kubáček, head of the Musem Documentation Centre, who has permitted reproduction of photographs from his family collection, and to Jim Horsford of the Czech & Slovak Railways Group for preparation of much of the narrow gauge material*. With acknowledgement also to the many friendly and helpful railwaymen and women of the ŽSR. Photographs are credited after the caption.

SLOVAKIA: A Land of Rivers, Mountains, Forests and Railways

Slovakia or the Slovak Republic is an independent country in central Europe with an area of 49,014 sq. kilometres and a population of approximately 5 million. It has common frontiers with Poland, Ukraine, Hungary, Austria and the Czech Republic, making for an interesting variety of international railway traffic. The capital of Slovakia is Bratislava, home to about half a million people, and in former times the capital of Hungary.

The Slovak landscape is mostly mountainous, with large areas of upland forest and lowland agriculture. The whole north of the country is formed by three spurs of the Carpathians, of which the northernmost and most beautiful part is formed by the peaks of the High Tatra Mountains. Gerlach, the highest rises to 2,655 metres (8,788 ft). South of the High Tatras (Velké Tatry) are the Low Tatras (Nizké Tatry), separated by the river Váh. Other principal mountain ranges are the Small and Great Fatras (Malá Fatra, Vel'ká Fatra), and the Slovak Ore Mountains (Slovenské Rudohorie). Surrounding most mountainous areas are ranges of hills, whose heights slope down to plains and the River Danube in the south and south-west.

The presence of mineral deposits in the hills and mountains resulted in early wagonways to serve mines. Naturally, a country rich in ores also has steelworks and other metal processing industries, including shipbuilding - Bratislava is a prominent Danube port. Slovakia also has rich farmlands providing staple foods, and in the south are vineyards supplying grapes for the winemaking industry. Forestry is widespread and constitutes

Looking north from Martin to the Malá Fatra hills beyond Vrútky, popular with local skiers. On 4th February 1998 passengers wait in temperatures of about -10 Celsius, as the 12:36 to Zvolen pulls in behind ŽSR Bo-Bo 750.128-1. Photo: Paul Catchpole

another part of the economy that led to the development of railways, mostly narrow gauge, and nowadays contributes to the ŽSR's freight tonnage.

The southern border of Slovakia from Bratislava as far as Szob is formed by the Danube, which carries traffic to and from Vienna and Budapest. The river Morava marks part of the western border, from Hodonín until its confluence with the Danube at the Austrian crossing point at Devinská Nová Ves.

Three main river systems or their tributaries have sources in the Tatras, and flow eventually into the Danube. These are the Váh, Hron and Tisza, each of which has a relevance to the railways of Slovakia as their valleys formed the easiest routes along which to build railways.

The Biely Váh rises at Štrba and forms the dividing line between the Low and High Tatras. It is joined by the Čierny Váh from the Low Tatras at Liptovský Mikuláš and by the Orava at Kral'ovany. Along its route run the Košice - Bohumín Railway as far as Žilina, and the Váh Valley Railway as far as Leopoldov. The confluence with the Danube is at Komárno.

The Hron rises within a couple of kilometres of the Čierny Váh, just the other side of Kráľova Hol'a (1948 m), and so too does the Hnílec, a tributary of the Tisza. This watershed is the mountain to the north of the Zvolen - Margecany line between Červená Skala and Telgárt Pension, in fact the spiral at Telgárt runs through the lower slopes of the mountain. To the north of the Hron are the Low Tatras, and to the south the Slovenské Rudohorie. Railways were built along most of the course of the Hron, mainly to improve access to the minerals in the mountains, and form some of the most scenic lines outside the Tatras. The Hron meets the Danube at Štúrovo.

The third river system, the Tisza, rises in the Carpthians in Romania, but is fed by numerous tributaries from the Tatras eastwards, including the Hornád and Laborec, which each have railways running alongside and expresses on these routes named after them. The Tisza itself only just meets Slovakia, forming the border for a few miles at the far south-eastern corner before flowing through Hungary to join the Danube in Serbia.

One other river among the many is worthy of note, the Poprad, which rises in the High Tatras and passes through the town of that name. There the river turns north and the waters eventually find their way into the Baltic Sea at Gdansk.

The climate of Slovakia is generally mild, with an annual average temperature of 8 to 10 degrees Centigrade, but plenty of snow in the winter. Typically, the seasons are clearly defined, winters are mild, and summers warm. The average temperature in winter is about -5 degrees Centigrade, in summer about 20 degrees.

A Historical Perspective

Archaeological discoveries have proved that the territory occupied by the present Slovakia was inhabited from the earliest times. The Slav peoples began to settle in this region by stages in the fourth century A.D., at the time of the decline of the Roman Empire and of the Migration of Peoples. At the beginning of the 9th century the kingdom of Nitra was established, and grew to become the Great Moravian Empire. Slavic literature and culture flourished here and spread to other Slav peoples to the east and south of Europe. After the collapse of the Great Moravian Empire at the beginning of the 10th century the Slav tribes of Slovakia were gradually subjected to the Magyars and for a thousand years were incorporated in the polyglot Hungarian kingdom. With the establishment of the Hungarian state, the Slovak people were tied more and more closely through the feudal system and clerical order to the kingdom of Hungary.

Slovakia played an important part in the feudal Hungarian state. In the 11th and 12th centuries many market centres and settlements of craftsman had already arisen on its soil, growing over time into small towns. These were also added to by the mining towns. Nitra's significance as a cultural centre grew once more, and Bratislava (Pressburg), Kremnica, Banská Bystrica, Banská Štiavnica, Košice, Levoca, Prešov, Bardejov and other towns became free royal towns. It was mainly in these towns that the most valuable monuments of Romanesque, Renaissance and Baroque architecture, sculpture and painting were preserved.

In the age of feudalism two great wars were carried into Slovak territory. In the middle of the 13th century the country was overrun by Tartar hordes and in the 16th and 17th centuries the Turks invaded southern Slovakia. Through an agreement made when the Habsburg Holy Roman Emperor had to save the country from invaders, Hungary, and Slovakia with it, were incorporated into the Habsburg Empire when the line of succession to the Hungarian throne was broken. The Emperor of Austria was crowned the King of Hungary, thus establishing the Austro-Hungarian Empire.

Throughout the era that followed, the life of the subject Slovak population was hard and the fight against feudal subjection often broke out into open rebellion. Latin was the official language of Slovakia during this period, but in writings and also in economic life the Slovak adaptation of Czech language was used as well. This fact and the lively economic and cultural relations between Slovakia and the Bohemian provinces, kept alive the consciousness of the common ties which united the Czechs and the Slovaks. The Slovak language was formed and grew in the 18th century, and the national consciousness grew in the 19th century, becoming a national movement, primarily as a reaction against Hungarian suppression.

The interval between 1849 and 1918 is one of the saddest periods of Slovak history. Every national expression was brutally suppressed. For most of this period the Slovaks had no cultural institution, no intermediate schools and almost no primary schools of their own. This political suppression was profoundly interwoven with the economic and social repression of the Slovak people, and the resulting hard economic and social conditions were the cause of mass emigration. In the struggle for the maintenance of the national consciousness the Czechs and the Slovaks came closer together.

The origins of the locomotives on shed at Bratislava main depot after the Second World War are indicative of Slovakia's history - a Hungarian class 324 2-6-2 adopted as ČSD type 344.4, and an ex-DR class 64 2-6-2T, ČSD 365.4.
Photo: Courtesy of ŽSR.

With the disintegration of Austria-Hungary at the end of World War I, the independent republic of Czechoslovakia was proclaimed by Czechs and Slovaks and developed as a Western-style democracy, becoming one of the top ten economies of the World during the inter-war period. In World War II Czechoslovakia was separated, and and on March 13th 1938 Slovakia established an independent pro-Nazi Slovak State, whereas the Czech part was occupied by Nazi Germany. Ruthenia declared independence at the same time as Slovakia and was invaded by Hungary the next day, then in November 1938 Hungary annexed large areas of southern Slovakia.

The national resistance movement in Slovakia culminated in the Slovak National Uprising in August 1944, in which members of the Communist party and Slovak National Partisans played a large part in the building and operating of armoured trains. The fate of Czechoslovakia was sealed at the Yalta Conference, held between the major Allied powers' representatives in February 1945. There it was decided that Czechoslovakia should fall within the Soviet sphere of interest. and that the majority of the country should be liberated from the Nazis by Soviet troops. After World War II Slovakia's borders were re-established but the Ukrainian part of Czechoslovakia, including Ruthenia, elected by plebiscite to join the USSR.

In 1946, the Communist party was elected to power. An absolute majority was gained at the beginning of 1948, as a result of which Czechoslovakia became part of the Soviet block. In 1968 an attempt by intellectuals represented by the Communist Party leader Alexander Dubček to create 'Socialism with Human Face' was crushed by an invasion of Warsaw Pact troops. Dubček and other moderates were purged and the staunchly pro-Soviet Gustav Husak put in control. Also in 1968, Slovaks were given greater autonomy and Czechoslovakia became a federation of two republics - Czech and Slovak.

The pro-Soviet regime collapsed in November 1989 during the widespread upheavals in Eastern Europe, and former dissident playwright Václav Havel was elected as president. The new government embarked on a program of democratization and the introduction of a free-market economy, however, under the pressure of Slovak political leaders, the Czech and Slovak federation was dissolved, and the two republics became independent on 1st January 1993.

During the Communist period locomotives of all types carried a red star. Many were removed during the Dubček era, only to be replaced, but in 1989 they were all removed (though by then steam had been gone nine years). Now that the the political situation has changed, these rather attractive embellishments can be seen again on some preserved locos. Sporting the largest type of star in June 1960, ČSD mixed traffic 4-8-2 no. 475.126 heads out of Bratislava with a heavy freight.
Photo: A.E. Durrant.

National Heritage

Much of the national heritage documenting the development of society from ancient times up to the present has been preserved in Slovakia, and this practice is being continued in the field of railways by the ŽSR's Museum and Documentation Centre.

Numerous important archaeological finds and localities which are not only being protected and restored, but also given their place in contemporary life, remind us of activities in the earliest periods of man's existence. Some have become parts of tourist

Zvolen castle is a well-known photographic landmark, though nowadays the scene is cluttered with overhead electic equipment. In this shot taken perhaps in the late 1940s, a 534.03 class 2-10-0 heads east with a train of vans.   *Photographer unknown.*

and "instructive" paths, others house museum expositions. These sites include Čertova Pec (Devil's Oven) at Radošina, a cave settlement from the Middle Palaeolithic period, and the Prepoštská Cave in Bojnice, also the home of Palaeolithic man. At Kyjatice is a Bronze Age urn cemetery, and at Ducové, near Piešt'any, an ancient Slav fortification settlement remains. Evidence of the Romans can be found at Rusovce-Gerulata near Bratislava, where there are the remnants of a Roman military post.

On the sites of ancient fortified settlements, large complexes and castles were usually built by Slovak ancestors. Most of them have been or are being restored, and converted into museums and galleries; the best known of these castles are Devín, Nitra, Trenčín, overlooking the station, Bojnice, Orava Spiš, Krásna Hôrka and Banská Štiavnica, but the complete list is much longer. The Bratislava Castle complex houses expositions of the Slovak National Museum and is also the seat of the Slovak National Council.

In several districts, whole complexes of valuable folk architecture have been preserved. The finest of those locations, some of them unique in design and construction for a variety of former uses, have been declared protected areas. The best known protected complexes of folk architecture are Cimcany, Vlkolínec, Podbiel, Ždiar and Osturňa - all with perfectly preserved timbered houses; remarkable dwellings and workshops of an Anabaptist community can be admired at Velké Leváre, a mining community in Špania Dolina, cave dwellings in Brhlovce, and a group of vineyard houses in the locality of Stara Hora (Old Hill) in Sebechleby. Several other valuable complexes of folk architecture are to be declared protected historical areas in the near future.

Many unique examples of folk architecture which lost their original environment or ceased to fulfil their functions have been transferred to open-air museums, skansens. In several of them, visitors can see demonstrations of old skills and technologies (mills, sawmills, fulling mills etc.). The most remarkable museums of folk architecture are in Martin (Slovak folk architecture in general), Zuberec (architecture of the Orava region), Vychylovka (Kysuce region), Pribylina (Liptov region), Bardejov Spa (Saris region), Svidník (Ukrainian culture), Stará L'ubovňa (Spiš region) and Humenné (Zemplín region).

Also numerous in Slovakia are technical monuments, mostly old ore mining and processing facilities in the Slovak Ore Mountains. Some of these relics have been moved from their original sites to open-air museums. The museum of mining in Banská Štiavnica is a unique institution; another technical monument in the vicinity of this ancient town is a complex of water reservoirs, a few of which still serve their original purpose in ore extraction operations. Most of these man-made lakes are now used for recreational and sport centres (Počúvadlo, Klinger, Banský Studenec). These reservoirs of considerable historical and cultural value enhance the scenic beauty of Štiavnice Hills.

Other technical monuments in Slovakia include water-powered hammer mills and narrow-gauge forest railways. Now in museum operation are the transport installations at Čierny Balog to the south of the Zvolen-Margecany line and Vychylovka in the Kysuce district. The latter is associated with the nearby open-air 'Muzeum kysuckey dediny' previously mentioned, where there is also a unique system designed for a great vertical drop in the mountains between the Orava river and the Kysuce. These technical monuments represented in their time important progress in engineering and other fields of technology.

On the Hronec Forestry line at Čierny Balog in September 1992, 760 mm gauge 0-6-0T no. 5 is at work with a varied selection of rolling stock.
Photo: John Scrace.

Preserved on a plinth at Brezno depot is 0-8-0T no. U46.901 from the Povážska Forestry Railway. Another example of this type works on the Vychylovka museum line.   Photo: D. James Horsford.

THE FIRST RAILWAYS IN SLOVAKIA

A two horse-power passenger train of Slovakia's first public railway, Bratislava - Trnava - Sered'. Photo: ŽSR archives.

It is common to think of railways as being a product of the steam age, but wagons were running on rails since at least the Middle Ages, not only in Britain, but in other countries around Europe, and probably further afield. The earliest concrete evidence of transport by rail in Slovakia is an altar painting at the cathedral in Rožňava dating from 1513. The town is in a mining area and the painting shows a scene with miners and a truck on wooden rails.

The first public railway on Slovak territory was built from Bratislava to Svätý Jur, a distance of about eight miles, and was opened on 27th September 1840. Horses were used to pull carriages and wagons on iron rails, even though steam locomotives had made their debut in neighbouring Austria by this time. Construction was inspired by the Linz-Budweis Horse Railway and financed by a group of seventeen businessmen and landowners in Bratislava, which was then still the capital of Hungary. Their wish was to promote the city's fortunes at a time when they were flagging in the face of competition from Vienna. This was part of the reason behind using horse-power - they could buy Hungarian horses and keep the investment within Hungary or they could buy expensive locomotives from abroad.

In an interesting parallel with locomotive traction, the railway bought different types of horse for passenger and goods service. The 'passenger' horses were fast runners from the Hortobad area of Hungary which worked in pairs hauling two coaches about 40 km per day. The 'goods' horses were Steiers, also worked in pairs, pulling up to five wagons. All horses worked a rota of two days on, three days off, and would be changed every three hours or so, presumably to allow a break. Passenger horses were retired after four years and the heavy Steiers after six. At its height the railway operated 54 passenger horses and 64 goods horses.

From its inception the railway planned to operate 20 passenger coaches and 100 wagons, all with the general appearance and construction of horse-drawn road vehicles of the day. An 1863 inventory of rolling stock showed 22 passenger vehicles, 156 goods wagons, 2 snow ploughs(!), and 42 other wagons. Five years later a break-down was available giving 10 1st/2nd class coaches, 10 3rd class coaches, 34 vans, 112 open wagons for wood, 3 for coal and 8 for other materials. The proportion of wood-carrying wagons is explained by the quantity of firewood consumed by the population of Bratislava.

The track was built to standard gauge, but the actual rails were built of oak timbers with an iron strip 13 mm high by 60 mm

Bratislava's first railway terminus as it appeared after the start of steam haulage.

wide bolted to the top. This allowed for a maximum axle weight of half a tonne. The route was surveyed by Mathias Schönerer, the Austrian engineer behind the Linz-Budweis railway, and built with a maximum gradient of 3.1 $^o/_{oo}$ involving many cuttings and embankments. Numerous wooden bridges were necessary, and some stone viaducts were also built.

The Bratislava terminus of the Horse Railway was built on the corner of Legionárska and Krížna streets, and still stands today, although well over a century has passed since it was used as a station. For many years the building had been in a run-down state, but the owners, Hydrostav a.s. were persuaded not to demolish it (as they had been considering in the 1980s) due to the building's historical importance. Instead the company embarked upon renewal of the structure and conversion to a cultural centre, including a display of pictures and documents relating to the railway.

The Horse Railway proved an initial success and the line was extended to Trnava, a distance of over twenty miles, inaugurated on 3rd June 1846. On 1st November that year another nine miles to the final terminus at Sered' were opened. Passenger trains between Bratislava and Trnava were operated twice daily in each direction, taking about three hours to complete the journey, depending on the condition of the horses and the weight of their load. Other services were run to Šenkvíc, situated 7.5 km outside Bratislava.

Eventually progress overtook horse traction and the railway, never having generated sufficient profit to convert to locomotive haulage in spite of being well patronised, was sold via a Parisian bank to the Vág Valley Railway, of which more presently. The last horses were retired on 10th October 1872, and after rebuilding the track with normal rails able to take the weight of locomotives, steam traction started in May the following year.

Sered' station on 4th October 1997, 125 years after the horses retired. The 'Motorák' railcar on the left has just brought in the local passenger service from Trnava, and a freight waits to proceed in the Leopoldov direction behind ČKD-built hood unit 742.124-1. Note the typical ČSD platforms - raised on one side, but sloping down to the rail on the other.   *Photo: Paul Catchpole.*

Railway development in general was slow as Hungary was almost entirely agrarian at this time, but in the same year as the Horse Railway reached Sered' work started on the country's first steam railway. The Hungarian Central Railway was building a line to Vienna, joining up with an existing line at Gärnserndorf, from where a section was constructed to today's Bratislava hlavní nádraží (main station) via Marchegg. This line was opened on 20th August 1848. In 1870 a direct route from Vienna to Marchegg was opened and the section from Gärnserndorf closed. The 150th anniversary of the original route was chosen as the appropriate time to reopen a severed line from a rebuilt Bratislava Petržalka station to Kitsee, just over the Austrian border, in order to provide a new electrified route to Vienna. The re-opened section links into the Vienna - Budapest line at Parndorf (ÖBB).

Meanwhile, in 1850 the Hungarian Central Railway was building another line from Bratislava, but heading south-east to Štúrovo, where it would meet with an existing railway running through Vács, forming a more direct link to Budapest. The Bratislava hl. n. to Štúrovo section was opened on 16th December 1850. Norris locomotives were being built in Vienna by this time, as well as in America, and were used on the new route by the Hungarian Central.

Until the 1920 the Orient Express on its journey beyond Vienna ran through Bratislava and Štúrovo, but the Treaty of Trianon created too many new borders in this area when the Austro-Hungarian Empire broke up, so it was re-routed to cross directly from Austria into Hungary without passing through Czechoslovakia.

Bratislava main station as built by the Hungarian Central Railway. The building is now a ŽSR office and the former platform area is sidings, used until the mid 1990s to store some unrestored steam locos belonging to the national collection. Today's station building and the platforms are up the station approach on the opposite side of the old terminus.

Bratislava hlavní station more or less as it appears today, though electric locomotives would now stand in place of the unidentified class 344.4 2-6-2 and 387.001. The Pacific's tender gives the only clue to when the photo was taken, as it is a type introduced in 1937, but neither loco posesses a post-1948 red star.
Both photos: ŽSR archives.

THE VÁH VALLEY RAILWAY (Vágvölgyi vasút)

In a scene from 1883, a 2-4-0 is seen on the viaduct at Báhoň over a small tributary of the Váh. It seems the early British railways were not the only ones to show no consideration for the crew in a cab open to the elements. Photo: ŽSR archives.

Known in Slovak as the Povázská dráha, the V.V.V. runs from Bratislava to Žilina, where it meets the Košice - Bohumín Railway. Proposals to build a railway line from Bratislava to Žilina had been made as far back as 1856, backed by influence from the town of Nitra, where there was a wish to gain access to the world at large by building a line through Hlohovec to join the proposed railway. Unfortunately none of the proposals were backed by enough finance to get the project under way until the 1870s.

The Bratislava - Sered' Horse Railway had been bought out in 1871 by a French bank, and sold on the next year through the Wiener Wechselbank to the Vág Valley Railway. As the track had been built to standard gauge the route lent itself readily to conversion to locomotive haulage. Steam traction started as far as Trnava on 1st May 1873 although the section to Szered' was not converted until 1st September 1878.

The V.V.V. was opened in stages as far as Trenčín by 1st May 1878, the section inaugurated on this day being that between Trenčín and Nové Město nad Váhom, where there is a carriage works. Each stage up to this point had had its own financial problems, simply caused by the need to find investment rather than by any practical problems, so construction beyond Trenčín was undertaken by the Austro-Hungarian State Railways (StEG/ÁVT), who took over ownership of the line and finished the route via Púchov to Žilina. Public services through to Žilina commenced on 1st November 1883, the same day as the start of steam traction from Trnava to Sered'.

The railway does not actually reach the vicinity of the river Váh until Leopoldov, and then runs with the river some distance off to the east of the line as far as Trenčín. Just before the station the tracks turn and cross over the Váh below Trenčín Castle, and from here to Žilina the line follows the river more closely. The terrain as far as Púchov is unspectacular, with farms in the broad valley and the sight of hills in the distance, but the view from the carriage window becomes more interesting as the railway approaches Žilina.

Heavy freight 2-10-0 no. 534.094 at Trenčianska Teplá depot on 27th September 1968. This particular loco, built by ČKD in 1937, was the first of the modernised version of class 534.0. Note the tender piled high with coal - these locos demanded hard work of their firemen, but were hard sloggers themselves in return.
Photo: Jan Koutný.

The first locomotives for the V.V.V. came from Sigl's works in Vienna, and were of two types corresponding to MÁV classes 238 and 335, 2-4-0 and 0-6-0 respectively. Three of the 2-4-0s were supplied, having become available from a cancelled order from an Italian railway, and eight of the 0-6-0s were built to order for the opening of the Váh Valley Railway. Later on standard MÁV types were employed.

In 1904 the line from Leopoldov to Žilina was doubled, but it was not until the 1940s that double tracks were laid south to Bratislava as trains were routed from Leopoldov through Galanta to reach the capital. The importance of the line as part of the express route to Košice led to electrification in the 1980s, and in fact the mileage to Púchov was electrified first, along with the KBD, using 3 kV DC. The lines from Galanta to Leopoldov and Trnava via Sered' were in fact electrified next, before the rest of the Váh Valley route, but using the 25 kV AC 50 hz network that extended through southern Czechoslovakia. The final link between Púchov and Brunovce was energised on 28th January 1988 also on 25 kV AC. All Czechoslovakian electric locomotives built in modern times (i.e. since the E499.0 'Bobina' class of the 1950s) have been supplied by the Škoda works in the Czech town of Plzeň.

In order to work through beyond Brunovce the locomotives used have to be dual-current types, recognisable by a blue livery, normally with a broad yellow band. The first of these were the 160 kph (100 mph approx.) ES499.0 built in 1974-75 by Škoda, all now on the ŽSR, and all shedded at Bratislava. As well as working to Žilina and beyond, this class is also used on international trains to Prague, which is at the other end of the DC system that traverses the whole of the north of the former Czechoslovakia. The ČSD renumbered the ES499.0 Bo-Bos as class 350 in 1989 re-classification.

A more modern series of dual-current electrics is the 'Pershing' class, reputedly so called as they supposedly contain as many micro-chips as a Pershing missile! These are the 120 kph ES499.1, now class 363. A program of improvements has been put in place to bring the service speed up to 140 kph, and locomotives so treated are renumbered as class 362. Like the class 350, all are shedded at Bratislava.

Electric locomotives only working as far south as Brunovce are DC types, painted in green liveries, and described in the section on the Košice - Bohumín Railway, where they first worked. Electric locomotives on the southern section carry red liveries showing that they work on the AC system, either red and white, as originally turned out, or plain red with a yellow band.

The first AC type in Slovakia was the S499.0 (240), known popularly as the 'Laminatka' class from the laminated plastic and glass fibre material used to make the body. The series was built 1968-70, and split between České Budějovice and Bratislava for working expresses up to 140 kph. A freight version (S489.0/230) is shedded at Brno (ČD), so the Slovak 240s handle all types of traffic except shunting.

Shunting on AC lines, and also some trip freight working, is rostered to the class 210 (formerly S458.0). The type was specifically designed for such duties, and features a centre cab between low hoods, and covers over some electrical equipment sloped down in the fashion of the tanks on some steam shunters.

The 'Pershings' exist in an AC version, as well as the DC and dual-current models. Twelve examples of the 263 (S499.2) were turned out in 1987, all but two inherited by the ŽSR, and allocated to Bratislava depot. The maximum speed is 120 kph and they can usually be seen heading passenger trains.

In October 1997 'Laminatka' class leader 240.001-8 stands in Bratislava main station with IC 530, the 'Hron', awaiting departure to Banská Bystrica.
Photo: Ing. Juraj Greguš

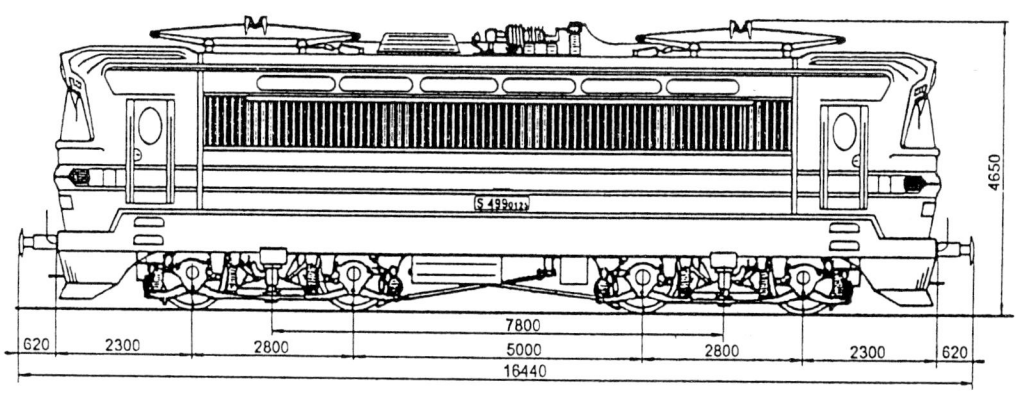

THE ÁVT - Austro-Hungarian State Railway Co.

After the Hungarian uprising in 1848 the Habsburg Emperor Franz Josef I decided upon a programme of nationalising the railways. The Hungarian Central Railway was the first to be taken over, on 7th March 1850, following which it was renamed the Südöstlicher Staatsbahn. The emperor changed his mind and the state lines were sold to a company known in Austria as the StEG (Österreichische Staats Eisenbahn Gesellschaft), and in Hungary as the ÁVT (Osztrák-magyar államvasút társaság). The Hungarian part of the ÁVT was absorbed into the MÁV in stages by 1st January 1891. Most of the ÁVT's lines were in other parts of Austro-Hungary, and only a few reached into Slovak territory.

The ÁVT built or took over a number of lines in south-western Slovakia, including the Váh Valley Railway. A line from Palárikovo to Šurany was opened on 15th January 1874, and from there an MÁV-built extension continues on to Zlaté Moravce (opened 7th Sept 1894). In 1876 a new route starting at Šurany and heading north through Nitra was opened in stages. Nitra is a town of some importance, commercially as well as in Slovakia's cultural history, and today boasts a container terminal.

THE TISZA DISTRICT RAILWAY

The Tisza district of the Dual Monarchy lies mainly in the north-east of today's Hungary, in an area through which the river of that name flows. After rising in the Carpathian mountains of Romania, the Tisza's course takes it to a point where the Ukrainian, Hungarian and Slovak borders meet. For about 15 miles the river marks the frontiers and immediately south of Chop turns south-west into Hungary, to cross the eastern plains and eventually flow into the Danube. In this area a network of light standard gauge railways were built, reaching Miskolc in 1859. From a junction just outside Miskolc a line was built through Barca to Košice, inaugurated on 14th August 1860.

The first locomotives on the TDR were four Norris 4-2-0s reputed to have been built originally for the Kaiser Ferdinands Nordbahn. It would be interesting to trace which these were, as none seem to have been sold directly from the KFNB, although they may have passed through a dealer or factory before re-sale. The Hungarian Central Railway certainly had Norris locomotives, though these were mostly built new rather than purchased second-hand.

With the exception of a pair of 0-6-0s which were too heavy for the track, the rest of the railway's motive power consisted of four-coupled types, 2-4-0s and 4-4-0s. These were probably quite sufficient for light trains in a flat landscape. None of the TDR's locomotives passed to the ČSD.

In 1880 the route to Košice was transferred to the MÁV along with the rest of the Tisza District Railway.

Košice station before reconstruction.

465.032, ex-MÁV 424.094, on a freight train at Košice, 9th May 1961. A part of the electrification train can just be seen beyond the locomotive, and signals visible include both slotted-arm semaphore and colour lights.
Photo: A.E. Durrant

THE HUNGARIAN NORTH EASTERN RAILWAY

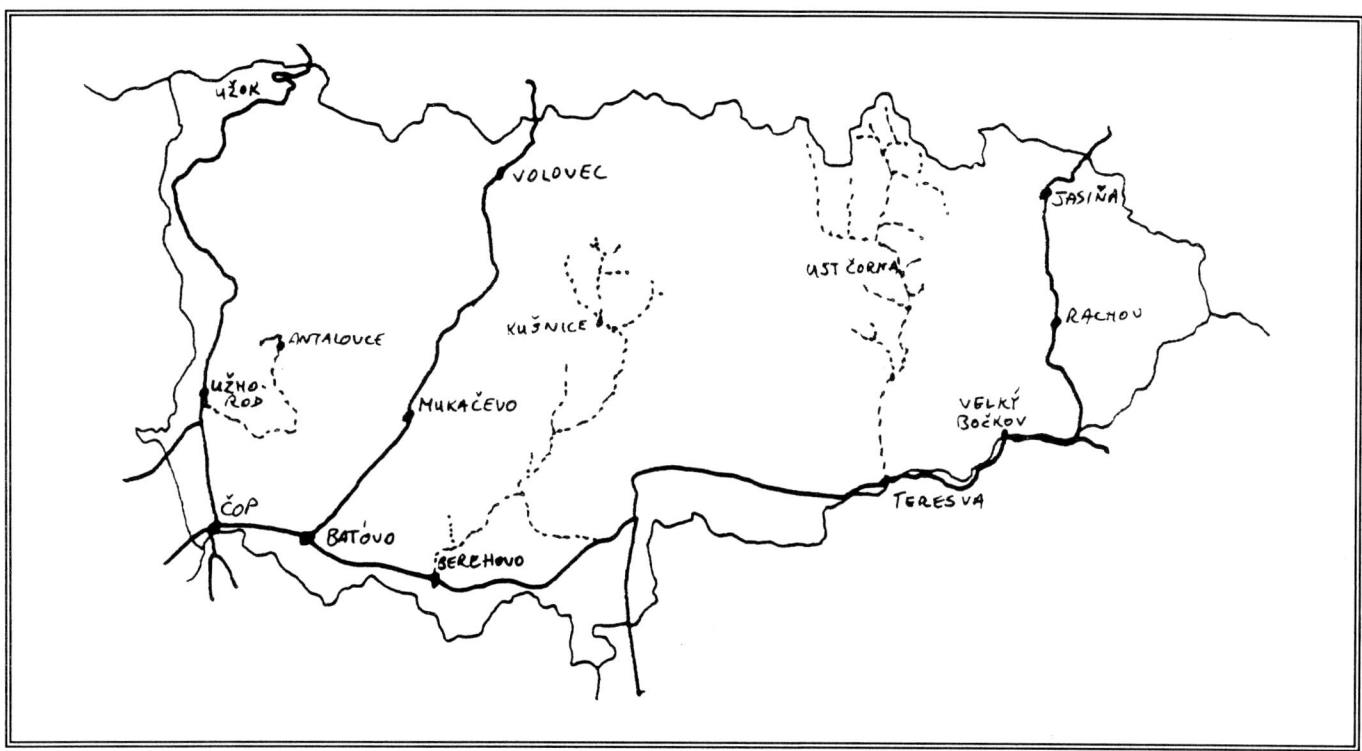

One of several lines starting as connections from the Tisza District Railways ran from Szerencs to Košice, crossing into Slovakia nowadays at Slovenské Nové Město. The line this far was opened on 26th October 1871, and to Michal'any on 7th January 1872. The Tisza District Railways were reached once more at Barca, just south of Košice, and trains started running into Košice on 22nd October 1872.

In an easterly direction construction of the line took it through today's border at Čierna nad Tisou to Čop (Chop), where another Hungarian North Eastern line joined from the south. From this junction onwards we're in Podkarpatské Rus - Sub-Carpathian Russia, which is now part of the Ukraine but was a part of Czechoslovakia and operated by the ČSD between the wars.

Construction of the line turned north from Čop to Uzhgorod, and saw the start of services from Košice on 25th August 1872. The MÁV was also building a line southwards from Lemberg (today Łvov), passing into Czechoslovakian territory at Užok and reaching as far as Velký Berezny. South of Užok there is a long stretch of tunnels, spindly viaducts and winding tracks descending from the Carpathian mountains. The Hungarian North Eastern and MÁV rails were connected in 1897 by the Uzh Valley Railway, a local line operated by four MÁV 0-6-0T, nos. 1-4, renumbered 377.484-487 in 1902 when absorbed into Hungarian stock.

The opening to Korl'ovo two months after the Uzhgorod route was significant, as another HNER line running from the Tisza system through the Romanian town of Satu Mare joined here.

Progress east was rapid, and two more sections were opened on the same day only a short while after the Korl'ovo stretch, on 4th December 1872. These were the main line to Sighet, now in Romania, and a secondary line from Bat'ovo, just east of Čop to Mukačevo. In the mid to late 1880s the MÁV built a line northwards from Mukačevo through the Carpthians at Beszkid to connect with the Lemberg-Czernowitz-Jassy Railway, and this became part of the ČSD as far as Volovec after 1918.

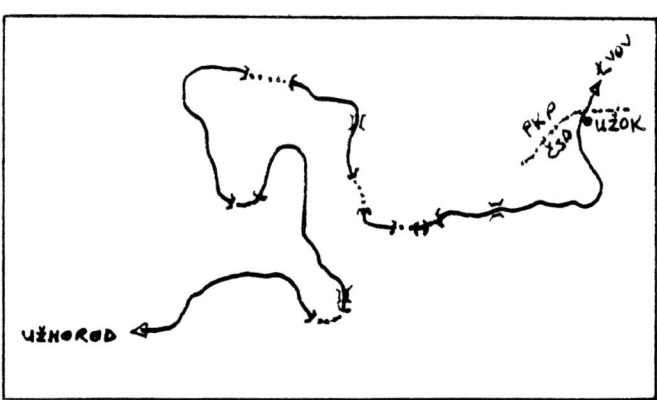

The section to Sighet was also extended, crossing back into Czechoslovakia at Trebušany and continuing through Rožňava to Jasiňa. A secondary line crossing from here into Galicia was the ČSD's most easterly point, and in fact during the inter-war period this part of Galicia was in Poland, although it is now part of the Ukraine. A ČSD express ran the full distance between Jasiňa and Prague until 1938.

17

The Hungarian North Eastern Railway was absorbed by the MÁV in 1890, but fell into the territories and separate railway administrations of Romania, the USSR and Czechoslovakia as well as Hungary when the new borders were drawn in 1918. After Sub-Carpathian Russia voted to became part of the USSR in 1946, the railways were converted by the SZD to 5' gauge (1524 mm).

As with other private railways in Hungary, the locomotives

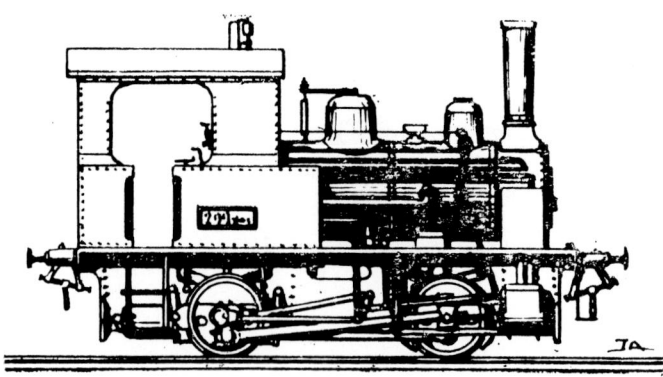

ČSD 200.001, drawn by Josef Janata for the 'Atlas Lokomotiv'

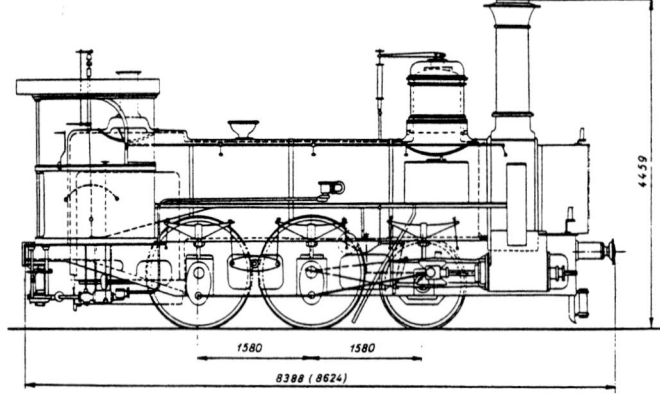

The Hungarian class 238 2-4-0. Courtesy MÁV.

were standard MÁV designs built at Budapest. The earliest types in use were 2-4-0s of class 238 and 0-6-0s of classes 335 and 374. In 1887 eight class 221 4-4-0s were added to the fleet, and a pair of class 377 0-6-0T in 1890. The latter were replacements for two compound 0-4-0WT built in 1884, the first compounds in Hungary, and prototypes of a series of twenty-four such tank engines. These little well tanks were not suitable for the tasks demanded of them and were sold to the Poprad Local Railway, eventually becoming ČSD 200.201/202.

The First Hungarian - Galician Railway

A link was made from the Hungarian North Eastern Railway at Michal'any to the Galician town of Przemysl. The first part of this was an easy run across the plains, passing through junctions at Trebišov, Bánovce nad Ondavou and Stráške, and serving Michalovce before reaching Humenné. The line as far as Humenné was opened on Christmas day 1871.

Beyond Humenné, however, the Carpthians had to be crossed. During 1872 construction of the line progressed in a southerly direction from Przemysl and was opened to Łupków that year, but it was not until 12th June 1873 that the line north from Humenné was opened to Vydraň (a few kilometres beyond Medzilaborce). This still left a gap of about 8 km at the summit of the line, with a tunnel to be bored, but in the spring of 1874 this final section was completed, and was inaugurated on 31st May.

The separation of the railway administrations of Austria-Hungary in 1889 resulted in the Austrian StEG taking control of the Galician section and the MÁV taking responsibility for the rest in Slovakia. During the First World War the line assumed a strategic importance as it was a link in the route from Budapest to the Lemberg-Czernowitz-Jassy Eisenbahn, which itself had been built to allow military access to the border with Russia on the Habsburg Empire's farthest frontier.

The First Hungarian-Galician Railway's motive power fleet was made up of MÁV standard types built at Budapest works. They found they could manage with class 238 and 241 2-4-0s and class 335 0-6-0s, but without class 441 0-8-0s, three of which were purchased and sold on later as surplus to requirements. Four of the MÁV's 441s were taken over by the ČSD, however, it's not known if these included any of those mentioned here. Modern traction on the line these days consists mainly of class 810 railcars and class 751/752 Bo-Bos.

From 1918 the summit tunnel beyond Medzilaborce marked the border between Poland and Czechoslovakia, the entrance in one country, the exit in another. Galicia passed to Poland and the railway from the tunnel to Przemysl became part of the PKP whilst the southern part was absorbed by the ČSD. Towards the end of 1944 the rail link through the tunnel was converted by the Soviet Red Army to the Russian 5' gauge from Poland as far as Humenné, however, it was converted back again two years later! A major overhaul of the tunnel was made at the same time, as it had been damaged at various times in two world wars, and re-opening with standard gauge track took place on 7th November 1946, on which occassion a ceremonial gathering watched 374.014 enter the tunnel.

In the early 1950s fighting was going on between Poland and the Red Army, so for Czechoslovakian security the tunnel was closed again. It was not until 13th June 1974 that services through the tunnel started once more, when the PKP and SNCFR wanted a standard gauge route to Romania, but in 1988 it fell out of use through lack of traffic.

With the end of Communism in eastern and central Europe a new opportunity beckoned. A meeting of representatives of the railways of Slovakia, Poland, Romania, and Ukraine was held in Łupków, for which the non-PKP delegates transported through the tunnel by a class 830 (M262.0) railcar. It was decided to arrange a standard gauge link from Łupków through to Halmeu in Romania, via the ŽSR and UŽ, involving adding a third rail to convert the track to dual gauge in Ruthenian area of the Ukraine. On 5th September 1995 the PKP and ŽSR started running trains through the tunnel, and today there is an international passenger, hauled on its Ukrainian leg by Voroshilovgrad-built 'Sergei' Co-Cos.

MAGYAR ÁLLAMVASÚT - MÁV

Hungary's lightweight 2-6-2T appeared in several forms, with and without compounding, superheating and Brotan boilers. ČSD 335.051, ex-MÁV 375.605, was a superheated simple with a conventional boiler. This particular example was of 1909 vintage, and still on former home territory nearly half a century later when seen at Komárom on 21st August 1968. Photo: A.E. Durrant.

The Royal Hungarian State Railways were formed in 1869 when the newly constituted Hungarian parliament took over the Hungarian Northern Railway and started to build new routes. Additionally, the MÁV took on operation of lines owned by other commercial concerns.

The Hungarian Northern's line from Hatvan was extended into Slovak territory in 1871, crossing the border near the villages of Šiatorská and Bukovinka. The first town of significance is Fiľakovo, after which the line passes through Lučenec and on to Zvolen. For the last 25 km or so this route follows the valley of the river Slatina into gradually hillier country, passing through Vígľaš. The opening as far as Zvolen took place on 18th June 1871, but the following year construction of a further extension was undertaken, with the eventual object of reaching Vrútky to join the Košice-Bohumín Railway.

The river Hron is followed as far as Hronská Dúbrava and a few miles further on, just before Stará Kremnička, the line turns north to wind its way through the Kremnické Vrchy hills. The section from here to Diviaky later required the use of Europe's largest Mallet locomotives, the 601 class 2-6-6-0s (ČSD 636.0).

Brotan-boilered 0-6-6-0 Mallet ČSD no. 623.006 suffered a mishap at Stará Kremnica in August 1927. This was actually one of the locos built for the Košice - Bohumín Railway, working off its own rails in more ways than one. Photo: Anon. Coll. Paul Catchpole.

The driver of Škoda DC electric 121.040-0 gives a friendly wave as his loco hauls a northbound goods train through the 'Turiec Garden' at Martin on 4th February 1998. This class of electrics were built in 1960, and operate on the 3kV DC system, now extended south from Vrútky on the former MÁV line to Zvolen. Photo: Paul Catchpole.

From Diviaky onwards the railway is in an area known as the 'Turčianská Zahradka' or 'Turiec Garden', where the broad valley of the river Turiec runs through a circle of mountains formed by the Malá Fatra and the Vel'ká Fatra. River and railway run through the ancient capital of Slovakia, Martin, meeting the Váh and the KBD at Vrútky. Public services from Zvolen to Vrútky started running on 12th August 1872.

Martin, formerly St. Martin, is the seat of Slovak culture, the Matice Slovenskej, and home of the Slovak National Museum. It is also where this publication was printed, at one of the country's leading printing houses, Neografia. Five minutes walk from Neografia are the offices of Martinská Mechatronická, where the class 755 reconstructed and modernised 'Goggles' type Bo-Bo was conceived and designed, and located on the western side of the river Turiec, only a few minutes walk further, is the former locomotive building works of the Turčianské Strojárne, today known as ŽTS Martin. Freight rolling stock is still built at this factory, and they produce other large industrial plant and machinery, but the plant is perhaps best known for the vast quantity of tanks turned out for the Eastern Bloc countries, particularly the Russian T.34.

Vrútky is very close to Martin, and is served by the same local bus administration and railcar shuttles. The railway works are the main reason behind the historical development of the town, which is also incidentally home to Nadas, the publisher of official and general interest transport books and magazines, including the ŽSR timetable.

Returning to the railway itself, three Hungarian 0-6-6-0 compound Mallets of MÁV class 651 (ČSD 623.001-003) were the first steam superpower on the line, supplemented by three of the MÁV 601s mentioned earlier (ČSD 636.0). In spite of their grand size and appearance (and how sad that none were saved for future generations), the ČSD's 534.0 class 2-10-0s proved just as capable, but more economical on coal, only requiring one fireman instead of two!

Later on the ČSD 556.0 2-10-0s were used, eventually giving way to diesels. Now, in the late 1990s, most freight is handled by class 770/771 Co-Co hood units, and passenger services either by the class 754/753 Bo-Bo 'Goggles' diesels or jazzily painted class 850/851 four-axle railcars and trailers. At the time of writing Vrútky is operating one of the last 'Sergei' class active in Slovakia, 781.312-4, generally on light freights, and often on the line to Zvolen.

A class 851 (M286.1) railcar and trailers stands at Zvolen. The Tatra Studénka works originally turned these units out 1968-69 wearing a much more tasteful red and cream livery. Their current red, white, yellow and two shades of grey would not be amiss on a wartime battleship as 'dazzle' camouflage! With a maximum speed of 110 kph, the 851s fall within the express railcar category. (3/1997).
Photo: Paul Catchpole.

Another line was built from Zvolen by the MÁV, northwards to the important regional town of Banská Bystrica. The opening took place on 3rd September 1873, but construction continued in an easterly direction to Podbrezová, inaugurated 28th July 1884. This enabled railway access to iron ore deposits in the valley of the Hron, and in fact the railway runs beside the river for its entire length. Any settlements of significance are situated in the valley, and the rest of the surrounding country is sparsely populated, mainly by farmers and foresters. Podbrezová itself, although only a small town, has been a centre for steel production for well over a hundred years, and is dominated by the rolling mills.

The MÁV carried on building up the valley of the Hron after the turn of the century, starting at Brezno-Halny on the line to Pohronská Polhora. This took the railway as far as Červená Skala, which first saw public services on 28th November 1903. In later years the railway was extended through to Margecany, of which more presently, and the line as a whole is regarded as one of Slovakia's most scenic and photogenic. On the northern side of the route lie the Low Tatras, whilst to the south are the Veporské Vrchy range of hills, and in the middle are the railway and the river, with a road alongside providing easy access to locations for filming and photography.

Another route was opened in 1873, exactly a week after the Zvolen - Banská Bystrice line, from Banréve through Jesenské to Fil'akovo, where it met the 1871 line to Zvolen. This was not originally an MÁV line, but was part of an industrial and mining concern, the Gömöri iparvasutak, which owned extensive industrial railways in northern Hungary, operated on their behalf by the MÁV.

The Gömöri company was interested in exploiting deposits of iron ore, tin and lead in Slovakia and extended their network in 1874 from Jesenské to Tisovec, passing through Rimavská Sobota. As with other railways in mountainous country the line followed the easiest route alongside a river, in this case the Rimava, climbing for most of the way as it made its way up to the southern side of the Veporské Vrchy hills.

Ore from Tisovec was sent to blast furnaces at Hnúšt'a, about a

The second of the 0-8-2 Rack Tanks for the Tisovec - Pohronská Polhora line, used for posing a staff photo, thought to be at Brezno, prior to the 1911 re-numbering. Photo: Kubáček family collection.

third of the way back down the line to Rimavská Sobota, and the iron then had to reach the steelworks at Podbrezová. This involved an extremely long journey all the way round via Jesenské and Zvolen, a distance of almost 200 km in order to reach a destination only about 40 km away.

The MÁV built a more direct route via Brezno, but it involved crossing a very mountainous area with a sharp descent down to Pohronská Polhora. A gradient of 1 in 20 meant that installation of an Abt rack was necessary, and three 0-8-4 rack tanks were ordered specially from Floridsdorf for the opening of the rack section on 30th November 1896. A fourth was supplied in 1900. The original numbers were 4281-4, changed to 41.001-4 when the MÁV renumbered, and changed again by the ČSD, becoming 403.501-504. During the Second World War one of the viaducts was damaged and 403.503 was destroyed by partisans. It was 1946 before trains could run through once more, but after 1955 the line was only used for passenger trains so the rack tanks saw little use after this time and by 1964 they had been cut up.

The ČSD had some rack diesels built by SGP of Graz, Austria for the Tanvald-Harrachov line in northern Bohemia, but these were not put into service on the Tisovec-Pohronská Polhora rack, even though it was renewed 1964-65. Steam traction was superseded by adhesion diesels and railcars. The M131.1 four-wheel railcars built from 1948 onwards were used over the branch, superseded later by the M240.0 bogie railcars, class 820 as they are known today. The rack, however, was not removed, and when the track was re-laid in the early 1990s (and freight services reinstated) the rack was put back too - in spite of the fact that Slovakia has had no standard gauge rack traction since the demise of the steam locos! This may in fact be very fortunate. Firstly, 426.001 from the Tanvald-Harrachov line, (now a museum loco) was able to visit the Slovak line for its centenary, and secondly, the ČD has a Floridsdorf 0-8-2RT developed from the Slovak rack tanks under restoration and no rack line to run it on.

Another Gömöri line was pushed north in 1874, starting at a junction by the village of Lenartovce, which today is the first Slovak station over the border from Banréve. The railway follows the river Slaná almost along its entire length from Lenartovce to the end of the line at Dobšiná. Rožňava was briefly the terminus, from its opening on Mayday 1874 until the 26 km extension to Dobšiná was finished and inaugurated on 20th July that year. On the map it seems as though it almost meets the Zvolen - Margecany line, but this section did not exist at the time the branch reached Dobšiná.

Two other branches diverge from the Lenartovce - Rožňava line and head into the hills. They both leave the main line from a junction at Plešivec, one going 41 km to Muraň and the other 26 km to Slavošovce. Opening dates were 22nd November 1893 and 12th November 1894 respectively.

Services on such minor branches as these are painfully slow, that is if you want to get somewhere as opposed to enjoying the scenery - a journey to Slavošovce will take you a little over 45 minutes and to Muraň around an hour and a quarter (each way).

The line from Zvolen to Banská Bystrica turns north through the town. Slovak-built 'Čmelák' Co-Co 771.155-9 crosses a road near the town centre, having just run light engine through Zvolen Mesto station.
Photo: Paul Catchpole.

It must be said though that the pace of life is less frantic than in some other parts of Europe and rural train services do serve the community as they rightly should, and as many of us in other countries wish they did.

From the second half of the 1880s the MÁV engaged in more construction across the flat country of south-western Slovakia. Štúrovo was connected to Šahy on 24th September 1886, and 18th September the next year, a junction on this line at Čata enabled a link to Levice to be opened. From Šahy the railway was extended to Balassagyarmat in 1891, meeting a line being built south from Lučenec. After independence most of the line was marooned in Hungary, with Šahy just inside the border at one end and the village of Kalonda at the other end.

An added complication since 1989 has been that part of the way along a branch crossing back into Slovakia was built to serve Vel'ký Krtíš. This was relatively recent development, dating from the Communist period and opened on 30th May 1978. To get round the difficulties posed by this situation trains were being run over the Hungarian side of the border as nonstop 'corridor' services, thus avoiding customs formalities. This arrangement, however, has lapsed since the ČSD was split between the ČD and ŽSR, and today trains terminate at Kalonda, just 10 km south of Lučenec.

A much more important line was constructed from Devinská Nová Ves in 1891. The work was started by the StEG, but it actually came under authority of the MÁV by the time it was

Steam in the snow at Lučenec on 27th February 1971. 431.006 is one of the ÖBB class 93 2-8-2Ts built for the 1938-45 Slovenské Železnice when new locos were unavailable from Czech factories. One of these SŽ locos, 431.014, has survived as it was used in a film about the partisans' armoured trains and afterwards was stuffed and mounted at Zvolen.
Photo: Jan Koutný.

A pair of the ČSD's finest express engines, 498.109 and 498.114, roll into Bratislava with the southbound 'Balt-Orient Express' on 18th September 1963. Photo: A.E. Durrant.

opened on 27th October that year. The first 51 km as far as Kúty forms the greater part of the heavily used double-track main line to Břeclav (ČD) and Kúty is now a border station, as are also Holíč nad Moravou and Skalice na Slovensku. The railway is electified at 25kV 50Hz AC as far as Holíč and over the nearby border crossing to Hodonín. After the third border crossing the line continues in Moravia to Veselí nad Moravou and Uherské Hradiště. This border between the now separated Czech and Slovak Republics was once the dividing line between northern provinces of Austria and Hungary, and later kept Slovakia out of most of the Second World War.

A short branch to Stupava once left the main line at Devinské jazero, and was opened on the same day as the main line, but was closed at some time prior to 1940. There is not even a station there now. There are, however, two other branches that leave the main line at Zohor. The first goes 35 km through a series of villages to Plavecký Mikuláš, and the other goes 14 km to Záhorská Ves right on the Austrian border. Both were inaugurated in 1911, the Záhorská Ves line on 15th November and the Plavecký Mikuláš line on 9th December. It looks from maps as if there should have been a connection to the KFNB in Austria, about half a mile away from Záhorská Ves, but the author has been unable to find a reference to such a junction, and the long-established crossing at Marchegg is only a short distance away.

South of Bratislava the MÁV built a secondary line to Komárno across a flat, and in places, boggy area bounded on the one side by the Danube, and on the other by the rivers Malý Dunaj and Váh. The stretch of railway from Bratislava Nivy to Dunajská Streda (which means middle of the Danube), was opened on 23rd August 1895, and the remainder of the route on 17th November 1896. Two freight lines diverged en route to a couple of small towns close to the Danube, from Fakov to Šamorín and Dunajska Streda to Gabčikovo, only the second of which now survives. A third branch, with passenger services, was added later, built across an area of marshes and drainage canals to Kolárovo, operational from 8th November 1914.

After taking over ownership of the Váh Valley Railway a number of branches were built westwards by the MÁV. The first encountered on a northwards journey from Bratislava diverges at Trnava and forms a link through to Kúty. The first part of the journey crosses over the Malé Karpaty (Little Carpathians), passing through a tunnel about a kilometre long at the highest point, then descending to a junction at Jablonica in the valley of the river Myjava. Following the Myjava to Kúty, the railway serves Senice, the most important town on its route. The line was opened on 14th December 1897. From Jablonica a 12 km branch, opened on 6th September 1899, climbs to the small town of Brezová pod Bradlom, situated under Bradlo, the highest peak in the area (543 m). Also here is the grave of M.R. Štefánik, built in the traditional style of an edifice atop a small hill. Štefánik was one of the founders of Czechoslovakia in 1918.

Moving on north to Piešt'any there was once a short branch to Vrbové, with a spur serving the hamlet of Rakovice, both opened on 27th October 1906. The spur closed first, but the branch also closed some considerable time back.

Further on up the Váh is another line branching off at Nové Mesto nad Váhom, but this was built by the ČSD, and will be covered later. The next ex-MÁV line encountered is a branch between Trenčianska Teplá and Vlásky Priesmyk on the then Hungarian border, inaugurated on 28th October 1888. This was later extended by the ČSD to form a connection to a network of Moravian branches at Bylnice. The actual point where the line diverges from the Vág Valley Railway is half way between Trenčianska Teplá and Dubnica nad Váhom. After crossing the Váh it's all uphill as the line must go over the Bílé Karpaty (White Carpathians), passing between two peaks of over 600 m within 10 km.

Trenčianska Teplá is, however, best known for its 760 mm gauge electric railway to Trenčianská Teplice. This was never a steam line, but was built for electric railcar traction by the MÁV, and inaugurated on 27th July 1909, making it the first electric railway in Slovakia. A review of this line appears in the section on narrow gauge railways.

In 1901, a branch running south-east had been opened from Trenčín to Chynorany, meeting the lines being constructed in a northerly direction from Nitra. The first section from Nitra to Topol'čany was opened on 16th September 1881, through Chynorany to Velké Bielice on 19th August 1884, and on to Prievidza on 18th April 1896.

It was not until the early years of the 20th century that the line from Nitra to Prievidza was extended, but railway construction was still very much an on-going process until the 1914-18 war. On 31st October 1909 a branch was opened from Prievidza up the valley of the river Nitra to Nitrianské Pravno, a small town sitting below the southern tip of the Malá Fatra mountains. Afterwards a branch which now forms part of the through route to Horná Štubňa was laid into increasingly hilly terrain to Handlová, inaugurated 15th February 1913.

Just north of Nitra on the Topol'čany line is the village of Lužianky, mainly of note as a junction for routes heading off to Radošiná, Leopoldov and Zlaté Moravce. At Zlaté Moravce was a short spur to the small town of Topol'čianky, which opened on 21st September 1895 but was closed at some point before 1940. The Leopoldov branch through Hlohovec opened on 31st March 1898 forming a link to the Váh Valley Railway from Nitra, and this connection is still well used by local trains formed of railcars and trailers and by the occassional locomotive-hauled passenger and freight workings.

Radošiná is a small town in the hills forming the eastern side of the Váh Valley, and is reached by a branch following the rivers Radošinka and Blatnica. The branch does not actually start at Lužianky, but diverges from the Leopoldov line from the second stop along, Zbehy. The opening date was 26th November 1909. At the time of writing services are run by class 810 railcars and trailers to a timetable integrated with the Leopoldov line, so that trains to and from Nitra over the two routes are coupled to form a single train as far as Lužianky. As the trailers do not have driving cabs, this operation requires the use of a diesel pilot loco for a bizarre shunting operation.

From Leopoldov it is possible to travel via Sered' to Galanta on a line which these days is electrified, although local passenger workings still consist of class 810 railcars running under the wires. The southern end of the route from Galanta to Sered' was opened on 1st November 1883, and through to Leopoldov on 20th July 1885.

On 4th October 1997 Hlohovec station celebrated its centenary, and special trains were run over the weekend using newly restored 2-6-2T 331.027 with a rake of balcony-end four-wheelers. The anniversary special is seen heading for Leopoldov, having just departed from Hlohovec.
Photo: Paul Catchpole.

Left: ČSD 2-6-2 no. 344.404 was an ex-Hungarian two-cylinder compound, formerly MÁV 324.046. On September 18th 1963 the loco was photographed at the yard neck at Nové Zámky from an incoming train.
Photo: A.E. Durrant.

Below: Although built to a Hungarian design, ČSD 4-6-0 375.114 had never been an MÁV locomotive. It was one of a batch built by Henschel in 1918 to an order placed before the First World War that got diverted due to the reparations programme. The ČSD, however, put most of this class to work in former Hungarian areas, and 375.114 was seen at Komárno on 21st August 1958.
Photo: A.E. Durrant.

THE KOŠICE - BOHUMÍN RAILWAY

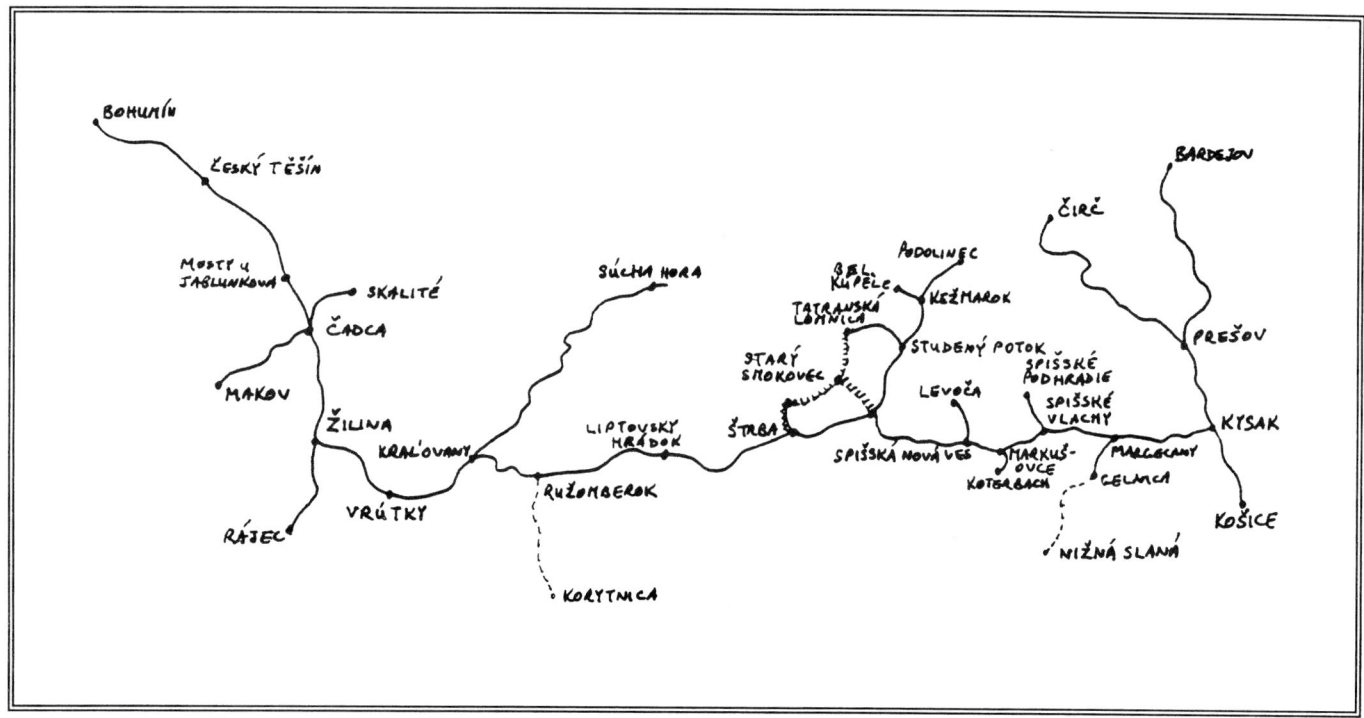

This, the largest of private railways in Slovakia started as a Hungarian concern, the Kassa-Oderbergi vasút, and was known in Czechoslovakia as the KBD - Košicko-Bohumínské Dráhy. The company was registered and managed from Budapest from its inception until 1st October 1921, by which time the ČSD had taken over. In addition to the general headquarters in Hungary there were two regional centres for traffic management, one in Těšín operating the section from Bohumín to Čadca and the other in Košice for the Čadca - Košice section. From Bohumín to Košice the overall distance is 429 km. In addition to its own main line, the KBD operated a number of local railways and branch lines on behalf of their owners, including the network of branches in the High Tatras. All these were laid after the KBD had been built, some of them as a result of being able to access to a main line.

Building took place in an east to west direction, starting at the coal and steel centre of Bohumín, near Ostrava on Moravia's northern border with Silesia. Here the Kaiser Ferdinands Nordbahn main line from Vienna divided to serve Wrocław and Kraków, both now in Poland. The expectation was that the presence of the KFNB would generate freight traffic for the new railway, especially minerals for Vítkovice steelworks. The first section from Bohumín to Český Těšín would serve the collieries of Karwiná on the way, ensuring an opportunity for earning substantial revenues as soon as the railway started operating. The line this far opened on 1st February 1869.

The terrain beyond Český Těšín became more difficult, but only a few miles further south was Třinec, another town with a huge steelworks. Although the railway was roughly following the river Olše (the Olsa), a climb was necessary to cross over the Beskidy mountains at the Jablunkov Pass. The ruling gradient is 17‰, (1 in 60), with curves down to 820 metres radius in order to gain an extra 408 metres (1,345 feet) of altitude in 53 km. The summit is reached at Mosty u Jablunkova, where there is a tunnel just short of the Slovak border.

The Jablunkov Pass was always the most difficult section of the KBD in terms of the demand placed on locomotives. For the opening of the line seven 0-6-0s for freight trains were bought from Sigl's works in Vienna, but the pass required something heavier. A number of MÁV type 326 0-6-0s were subsequently supplied to the KBD, but it was still necessary to use three of these to get a heavy train over the top. When a larger type of 0-6-0 became available from Budapest works, the MÁV class 325, six were allocated to the Silesian section of the railway and from then on two locos were able to manage.

In 1912 the KBD started using 0-6-6-0 Mallets of MÁV type 651 based at Vrútky. By this time the weight of goods trains had increased to the point where four 0-6-0s were needed over Jablunkova, and the introduction of the Mallets reduced this back to two. Nothing could beat the Mallets until the ČSD introduced the 556.0, a beast of a 2-10-0 able to take 4,000 tons at 25 kph on a level track.

Beyond Mosty u Jablunkov the line descends to Čadca, the first town of any size in Slovakia, and now the border point for international services to the Czech Republic. Two branches are operated from Čadca. The first is only just inside Slovakia, diverging to the north at Svrčinovec. This was built at the

27

The first of the KBD's 0-6-6-0 compound Mallets bearing it's ČSD number, 622.001, pictured about to go off on a turn as the driver is seen receiving his despatch orders. The guard's van behind is not so different from the ČSD design still in use today.
Photo: Anon., L.I. archive.

instigation of the Váh Valley Railway, but completed by the MÁV and operated by the KBD, services starting on 3rd November 1884. The line runs into Poland at Zwardoň, and from there the PKP has a connection through to Zywiec and thence Kraków. Today this is an important connection to the PKP, carring a couple of daily international expresses from Bratislava and a large volume of freight, not only bound for ŽSR yards, but also traversing Slovakia on the way to other countries.

The branch was initially worked by six 0-4-2 steam baggage vans built by Floridsdorf 1881-84, KBD numbers V.51-56 (ČSD 210.001-006). These little engines were capable of pulling several four-wheel coaches in spite of their diminutive size, but were displaced by larger locomotives and dispersed to other branches as traffic to Poland increased.

The other branch, from Čadca to Makov, was a much later addition to the network, opened to traffic on 9th July 1914. The line runs 26 km up the Kysuce valley, serving a series of villages strung along the route.

Beyond Čadca the KBD also follows the river Kysuca, as it twists its way to Krásno nad Kysucko. For visitors to the Východlovka open air museum and railway, this is the most accessible town that has a main road in the direction of Východlovka. From Krásno to Žilina the going gets easier, and the river Váh is crossed just before entering Žilina station. Trains heading in the Bratislava direction down the Váh Valley

Arriving under the tangle of wires at Žilina with a cross-border passenger service from Bohumín is a Slovak 3kV DC electric unit, no. 460.050-8, one of a series built for the ČSD by Tatra Studénka 1975-55, formerly class EM488.0.
Photo: Paul Catchpole.

28

Coming back down the ramp after a bought of hump shunting, is one of Žilina's centre-cab class 110s. The shunter is typically riding on the footsteps of the leading van, having stood on the other side of the hump uncoupling the wagons to be pushed over the top.
Photo: Paul Catchpole.

Railway without calling at Žilina have an avoiding line, mainly used by freights. Services between Bohumín and Žilina started running on 8th January 1871.

In addition to the convergence of main lines at Žilina, there exists a 21 km branch south to Rajec, opened on 10th October 1899. It is mainly a commuter line for Žilina, but also provides Žilina's citizens with a means of reaching a couple of minor spas and the Malá Fatra, where they may enjoy walking or skiing. The original motive power on this line was one of the outside-frame versions of the MÁV class 377 0-6-0T obtained when the KBD took over the Prešov - Tarnów Railway, KBD no. XII.530 (ČSD 310.510).

Just east of Žilina the Váh turns abruptly south under the railway, but is met again at Strečno, a most photogenic location. As the line and river turn south in a broad sweep, Strečno castle is seen perched high on a rock - an excellent vantage point, but not always open to the public. Two single line girder bridges take the double-track railway over the river and after a short

A period scene beside Strečno castle with an express hauled by one of the KBD's Südbahn type 4-8-0s.
Kubáčkovi collection.

29

Last of the Sergeis? 781.312-4 waits to take a rake of empty opens up the line from the yard at Vrútky in February 1998. Behind the loco is the works, ŽOS Vrútky, now occupying the site of the original depot, and more. Photo: Paul Catchpole.

embankment it disappears into a cliff. After emerging from the tunnel a few kilometres of scenery are passed on the way to Vrútky, where the MÁV route from Zvolen joined the KBD in 1872.

At Vrútky in 1871 the KBD established a locomotive works and depot. A clue to the traffic on the line is given by the locomotive allocation - 6 passenger locos and 24 for freight. The original depot was nearer the station than it is now, but larger facilities were required by the turn of the century and the works were also expanding. The present day depot was built 1900-1902 and the old one closed in 1904.

The main role of Vrútky works has always been overhaul and repair of locomotives, rather than construction, and this remains the case with regard to diesel and electric traction. There is still some work done on steam locomotives, as major restorations are shared mainly between Vrútky and Bratislava, though the lighter maintenance tasks will be carried out where the preserved locos are allocated - usually the shed where they were formerly in service.

Construction of the railway from Vrútky continued eastwards, crossing the Váh between Sučany and Turany in the wooded valley between the Malá Fatra and Vel'ka Fatra mountains. The line stays close beside the Váh, crossing the river Orava at Kral'ovany, from where a most spectacular branch follows the Orava to the present day terminus at Trstená.

The Orava Railway was built as a result of deputations from the local towns to the Government and the KBD head office in Budapest. The deputation was backed up by some local sponsorship in terms of money and materials, so construction went ahead.

From Kral'ovany the branch starts on north side of the KBD main line, and immediately encounters an obstacle - the mountain just past the end of the platform. After tunneling through the rock, the railway climbs steeply alongside the Orava through a forested cleft in the hills, twisting and turning with the river. At Párnica the gradient eases off briefly and the jagged peaks of the western end of the Tatras come into view. As the line progresses it continues to climb, passing through spectacular scenery, crossing tributaries of the Orava on numerous bridges.

The railway was opened in stages as building progressed, starting on 20th December 1898 with the 27 km to Oravský Podzámok, where the Orava Castle is situated just across the river. Three of the class XII 0-6-0T were employed to begin with, XII.527-529 (ČSD 310.507-509), but as construction progressed the XIIs were supplemented by a pair of Borsig 0-6-0T built in 1907, numbered as Orava Railway 4 & 5, later ČSD 310.701-702. 310.507 is preserved at Kuty, as part of the national collection.

'Pershing' 162.004-6 pulls into Kral'ovany station with a westbound express. The Orava branch passes through the base of the mountain behind the open wagon, and the peak towering behind is just across the Orava river.
Photo: Paul Catchpole.

Tvrdešín, reached by public services from 18th June 1899, is an alternative point from which to reach Výchylovka by road, though it is some distance. It is also the station nearest to the hotels and camp sites on the south of Lake Orava. Wilder shores of the lake are accessible within walking distance of Trstená. The railway was originally built beyond the present day terminus, to Suchá Hora right on the Polish border (in fact part of lake Orava is in Poland), and there used to be a crossing into Poland. The PKP section still remains as branch, but cutbacks may see it close.

310.701 drawn by Josef Janata.

Back on the KBD, the Váh is followed to Ružomberok, where until 1974 the picturesque station also served a narrow gauge line to the spa town of Korytnice. Beyond Ružomberok the main line follows a straight and level course until an 'S' bend takes it across a dam on the Váh and round Liptovská Mara lake to Liptovský Mikuláš. A few miles further on, after Liptovský Hrádok, the Biely Váh and Čierny Váh separate, and the KBD follows the former, climbing into the Tatras as it approaches Štrba. A long narrow gauge forestry railway once followed the Čierny Váh into the Low Tatras National Park, from Liptovský Hradok to Liptovský Teplička.

At Štrba the Slovak main line of the KBD reaches its highest point, 895 metres above sea level, before descending to Poprad. A metre gauge electric rack railway climbs from Štrba to the lake and mountain resort of Štrbské Pleso, and two more lines running into the High Tatras branch off at Poprad-Tatry and Poprad-Spišska Sobota respectively. The Tatra lines are described in their own separate section.

Climbing over the summit at Štrba presented another challenge to the motive power department, though not as severe as that presented by the Jablunkov Pass, and locomotive types suitable for the Silesian section were also shedded at Vrútky, Poprad and Spišská Nová Ves to cope with the 'hump' over the Tatras. Trains started running on the 138 km main line between Žilina and Poprad-Tatry on 8th December 1871, and four days later were able to reach Spišská Nová Ves, a fair achievement considering the distance, terrain, and construction methods available.

A few miles to the north of Spišská Nová Ves is the medieval town of Levoča, once the capital of 16 free German 'Zips' (Spiš) towns in this area of Slovakia. In the centre of the town original buildings and old town walls have been declared a cultural and

On the Kral'ovany - Trstená line at Párnica.

Above: In charge of freight on the Orava route is an immaculately turned out 'Frowning' (Zamračené) class Bo-Bo, 751.207-2, probably ex-works. These diesels have an unmistakeable burbling rumble, sometimes enhanced by the removal of the silencers by the driver specially for the sound effects! ČKD built the locos 1964-71, and the ČSD classified them as T478.1.

Left: Both the Czech and the Slovak railways are using some ultra-lightweight diesel and battery electric shunters built by ČKD for light station pilot and yard duties. A typical example is this little T212.0 that was out with a permanent way gang just beyond the station.   Both photos: Paul Catchpole, 4th February 1998.

KBD class XIIa (310.6) drawn by Josef Janata.

historical 'urban reservation'. A 12 km branch was built from here to the KBD at Spišská Nová Ves, the Levoča Valley Railway (or Löcsevölgyi vasút, as it was originally known in Hungarian), opened on 8th November 1892. 0-6-0T nos. XII.525-526 were operated by the KBD on behalf of the railway, later renumbered as ČSD 310.505-506.

The route of the KBD beyond Spišská Nová Ves is still through mountainous country, even though the Tatras have been left behind, and there are few straight kilometres of track before Kysak, although the gradients are easier. In fact the longest straight is in three kilometres of tunnel, through Suchý Vrch hill just east of Margecany. On the section from Spišská Nová Ves to Kysak the railway served copper and silver mines, and a steelworks at Krompachy.

Half way between Spišská Nová Ves and Margecany is Spišské Vlachy, junction for a branch to another of the Zips towns, Spišská Podhradie. Podhradie means below the castle, which is where the railway runs. The picturesque ruined castle is on a rise above the railway, within easy walking distance back from the station along a road to an excellent photographic location.

Three small 0-6-0T were purchased second-hand from the MÁV for the opening of the branch on 15th October 1894. They had been built at Krauss's Munich factory in 1884, works numbers 1396-1398, and carried KBD numbers XIIa.551-553. The ČSD renumbered them to 310.601-602. In the 1940s they were superseded by larger tank locos, but services on this branch and the aforementioned line to Levoča have for many years been run by bogie railcars of class M240.0 (class 820).

While the KBD was being pushed south and eastwards from Bohumín, a start was also made in the east of Slovakia with a route from Košice to Prešov. This was laid in a northerly direction through Kysak, following the river Hornád upstream and crossing over it in four places in the first 20 km. The railway opened on 1st September 1870, before the connection through the Tatras to Kysak had been made, but with the benefit of junctions with other railways that had reached Košice from the south. The line from Spišská Nová Ves reached Kysak and enabled through trains to be run between Košice and Bohumín from 18th March 1872.

An independent railway from Prešov to Tarnów (the Eperjes - Tarnówi vasút) was built north from Prešov into what was then a province of Austria, but is now Poland. For the first two thirds of the way to the junction at Orlov the line follows the river Torysa, but at Krivany a huge 'S' bend leads the railway into the valley of a minor tributary of the river Poprad. The next station after Krivany, Kamenice nad Torysou, is only two kilometres away as the crow flies, but the railway takes six!

The route as far as Orlov was opened on 1st May 1873, the same day as Bratislava - Trnava went over to steam traction. The northern section reached Orlov on 18th August 1876, and by the end of the year had been absorbed into the KBD, however, in 1879 the StEG took control of the part of the line lying on Austrian territory, and the MÁV did the same south of the border. This was simply one of those politicians' absurdities, as the line was completely isolated from the rest of the MÁV and the KBD continued to operate the line as before, using the same locomotives.

Along with operating responsibility for the Prešov - Tarnów Railway, a number of locomotives were taken over. Some of the XII class 0-6-0T have already been mentioned, but four were allocated to the Poprad Valley Railway (XII.521-524), and three others were re-located to the Prešov - Bardejov line, operated by the KBD from 1910: XII.531-533. The last of these, as ČSD 310.513, has been preserved at Vrútky. Five MÁV type 326 0-6-0s were also taken over by the KBD in addition to their own numerous and varied members of the class. They were absorbed into KBD class IIIb$_4$ and subsequently became ČSD 313.335-339.

Today there are three named expresses on the Prešov - Tarnów Railway, one of them the 'Prešovčan' running just between these two towns, and another, the 'Karpaty' travelling through four countries between Bucuresti and Warsaw. The link to Poland is of major importance for the ŽSR, as although the crossing at Medzilaborce has been reinstated, the Prešov - Orlov and Čadca - Zwardoň lines are the ones that carry the traffic. When in 1997 northern Moravia and the adjoining area of Slovakia suffered serious flooding, bridges and tracks to the west were washed out, so all the international traffic had to travel round the eastern end of the Tatras through Orlov.

The Bardejov - Prešov Railway, whose 44 kilometres were opened on 11th December 1893, was another independent concern absorbed into the KBD. For the most part the railway avoids climbing the hills in this relatively remote area, but has to wind its way round the contours from a point beyond the ruins of Kapušany castle, until it reaches Raslavice. Bardejov itself is one of the more significant towns of north-eastern Slovakia, boasting spa waters and preserved rural and town architecture. Traffic now in ŽSR days, however, is sparse: eight stopping trains a day each way from Prešov operated by railcars, plus an occasional freight.

Motive Power on the Košice - Bohumín Railway

The locomotive numbering system used was based on Hungarian State Railway's system. The basic classes are as below, with individual types differentiated by a letter after the number:

I	express
II	non-express passenger
III	goods
V	steam railcars
VI	heavy goods
X	shunters
XII	branch line engines
XIV	branch line engines
TVa	2-6-2T to MÁV 376 design

33

One of the original class IIIa 0-6-0s built in Vienna by Sigl to an order from the Belgian firm building the KBD. (Sigl 637/1868).
Photo: Jindřich Bek.

KBD Class	ČSD Class	Type	MÁV Class
I	253.1	4-4-0	-
Ia	254.4	4-4-0	220
Ip	354.9	4c/2-6-2	(KKStB 110)
It	455.0	4-8-0	(Südbahn 570)
IIa	221.0	2-4-0	238
IIb	232.1	2-4-0	-
IIIa	321.1	0-6-0	-
IIIb	313.3	0-6-0	326
IIIb$_3$	313.6	0-6-0	326
IIIe	313.2	0-6-0	326
IIIq	334.3	2c/0-6-0	325
V	210.0	0-4-2T	-
VIm	622.0	4c/0-6-6-0	651
X	200.2	2c/0-4-0T	-
XII	310.5	0-6-0T	-
XIIa	310.6	0-6-0T	-
XIIb	310.7	0-6-0T	-
XIVa	410.0	0-8-0T	475
XIVa	410.1	0-8-0T	475
TVa	320.2	2c/2-6-2T	376

Bridge testing near Hanušovce nad Topľou in 1943 with a pair of 2-6-2s rebuilt by the ČSD from the compound 354.9 class to superheated simple 365.3 in the 1930s.   Photo: Courtesy ŽSR.

A few other types were supplied specifically for the KBD during the ČSD era:

The ČSD class 623.0 was a Brotán boilered version of the class 622.0 compound Mallets, thirteen of which were ordered from the works in Budapest by the KBD, but not delivered until after independence, and hence never carried KBD numbers, but all went into service working mineral trains over the Jablunkov Pass.

Ten 2-8-0s were built by ČKD in 1924 and allocated to Žilina, but these were passenger locos with 1624 mm driving wheels, not freight locos. The class 455.1 was essentially designed as a Consolidation adaptation of the class 365.0 2-6-2 express locos, and proved to be an extremely capable and versatile locomotive. Even after displaced from their original duties, they were still able to manage freights and worked until 1964.

As new ČSD classes were introduced over the years, most of them worked over the KBD, as they were spread throughout the whole system, but particular mention might be made of some

An unidentified 4-8-0 of 455.0 class blowing off with the regulator shut as it passes a track gang. A wisp of steam from behind the chimney shows the electric generator is at work.

Photo: Courtesy ŽSR.

One of the Brotan-boilered 0-6-6-0 Mallets, ČSD no. 623.016, seen after a minor derailment at Frývaldov on 25th November 1937.

Photo: Anon., L.I. archives.

4-8-2s and 2-8-4s. These were the classes 486.0 and 486.1 respectively. Eight-coupled passenger locos were needed by the KBD from an early stage, and although the 486.0 was also used elsewhere, the KBD was the first to use it. The three 486.1s were the same as the 486.0, but constructed with the wheel arrangement turned round, influenced by the introduction of Austria's class 214. All three were based at Spišská Nová Ves, where demanding duties would enable a direct comparison of wheel arrangements to be made. In the end no advantage was found, and the subsequent 498.0 and 498.1 classes were built as 4-8-2s. From the late 1940s the 498.0 were working between Prague and Košice, and sharing turns on the same diagrams were the three class 476.0 3-cylinder compounds.

Class leader of the mixed traffic 2-8-0s, 455.101, speeds past Horný Hričov, just west of Žilina, where all ten were based. As built they were class 445.1, but a reclassification occurred when they proved capable of greater speed than expected. Note the drive onto the second coupled axle, but with valve gear actuated from the third. Also the cheery driver who has obviously seen 'Dusty' at the trackside!

Another rare 2-8-0, 436.002, runs through Dolný Hričov with a local goods train. This is also one in a class of ten, built by the Swiss firm of Winterthur in 1918 for the British Army's Railway Operating Department.
Both photos: A.E. Durrant, 19th August 1958.

Electric Traction on the KBD

The last classes built specially for the KBD route came after the steam era. Due to the importance of the connection from Prague to Košice, and beyond to the USSR, the KBD was the first main line electrified in Slovakia. The current used was and still is 3kV DC.

Liptovský Mikuláš to Spišská Nová Ves was the first part of the ČSD energised. Work started in 1954 and this first section was energised in 1955. The wires reached Žilina on 25th February 1956, but electrification proceeded westwards via Púchov to Horní Lideč, energised on 12th September 1961. The electricity from Košice south and east to Čop (over the Ukrainian border), was switched on throughout on 1st July 1962.

It was not until 1963 that the poles went up on the Moravian/Silesian part of the KBD. September 23rd 1964 finally saw Žilina energised from the west. Prešov was electrified much later, on 26th May 1978, at the same time as the 5' gauge to Užghorod was also being electrified. Later still, on 22nd November 1982 Vrútky to Martin was energised.

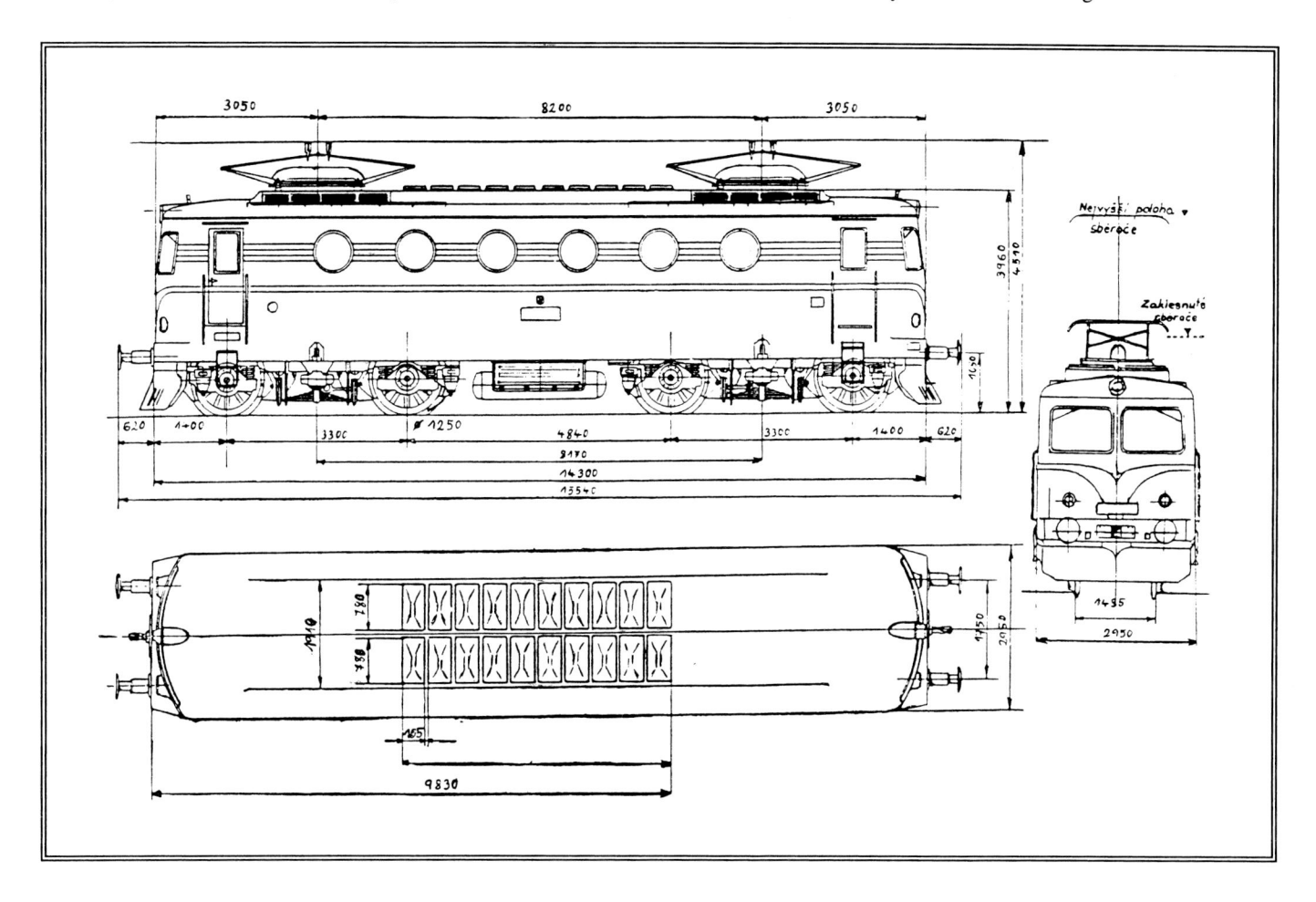

The first electric locomotives for the newly electrified system were the E499.0 (140 class) for passenger service. Development and construction took place at the Škoda works in Plzeň from 1953 onwards, under the leadership of ing. Hanyk, and since then Škoda has built all the ČSD's electric locomotives. The E499.0s were given a nickname 'Bobina', arising from the Bo-Bo wheel arrangement. The bogies were built under license from SLM as they were from the Swiss class Ae 4/4, and much of the rest of the technology was based on the Swiss electrics.

The first ten members of the class were given a blue and white livery with a silver flash and grey bogies etc. Green was then adopted for all DC locos, and blue was subsequently adopted to indicate dual current electrics, so the class was reliveried to two-tone green, and later to plain green with a yellow flash.

In service on the KBD the 'Bobinas' were a success, and as the class multiplied it spread to other parts of the ČSD's growing DC system. Technical developments gave rise to the E499.1 (141), none of which passed to ŽSR stock, and thence in 1960 to the E469.1 (121), a freight version of the E499.1 with lower gearing and ballasted for protection against wheelslip. On separation of the Republics 13 of the 85 locos passed to the ŽSR.

For the gradients of the KBD and the Czech main line at Česká Třebová it was decided that the heavy freights needed a Co-Co electric, and Škoda developed the prototype E669.0. Series production as class E669.1 took place in 1960-62, but the first

*ŽSR electric goods engines eastbound at Kraľovany, March 1997. Photos: Paul Catchpole.
Top: 184.064-4 of Košice depot. Above: 131.019-2 / 131.020-0 of Spišská Nová Ves.*

examples received by the former KBD were the E669.2 variant (now class 182), built 1963-65. Another variant was built in 1971, naturally the E699.3 (183), all of which were shedded at Žilina, Spišská Nová Ves and Košice.

In spite of the prodigious hauling power of the E699.x electric superpower was introduced in 1980 in the form of the E479.1 (131) twin units. Škoda turned these out between 1980 and 1982, and the ČSD allocated all 100 to Spišská Nová Ves, which is still their home depot on the ŽSR. The body shape, bogies, and much of the inside workings owe their design to the 'Pershing' class 162/163 passenger locos, some of which are also in service on the ŽSR. Today the 131s command freight trains throughout the former KBD and most of the linked 3kV DC lines, still as far as has been observed, paired together numerically as when supplied to the ČSD.

RAILWAYS IN THE TATRAS

The Poprad Valley Railway

Where the Košice - Bohumín Railway turns south round the outskirts of Poprad is the station of Poprad-Spišská Sobota, junction for the Poprad Valley Railway. It was built as a local venture, and operated on behalf of the owners by the KBD. The first section linked Poprad with Kežmarok, and was opened on 18th December 1889 with motive power provided by the two 0-4-0WT obtained in 1876 from the Prešov - Tanów Railway. These were later supplemented by four outside framed versions of the MÁV class 377 0-6-0T. The KBD numbers for the latter were X11.521-524, (ČSD 310.501-504).

Another 8 km were added taking the railway to Spišská Belá, open from 25th July 1892. When the branch was extended afterwards to Podolínec, the new section was started from a couple of kilometres outside Spišská Belá at Strážky zastávka, just a wayside halt. A new station was built at Spišská Belá zastávka on the new line and the short spur curving into the town was then closed.

Just short of Vel'ká Lomnica is a small river tumbles its way down from the mountains, the very aptly named Studený Potok, meaning cold stream. Next to it is the station of the same name from where a branch runs up right into the Tatras serving the ski resort of Tatranská Lomnica 850 metres above sea level. This was opened on 1st September 1895. The inclines were rather demanding on the 0-6-0T already in use and the KBD obtained from the MÁV five short-wheelbase, outside-frame 0-8-0T with Klein-Lindner axles, the MÁV class 475. To these were added another similar loco ordered specially from Budapest works in 1909. The first five carried ČSD numbers 410.001-005, and the other was 410.101, however, the differences were superficial and it was later numbered in the same series as 410.006. The 0-8-0T proved very capable on the gradients and worked the line until 1950, and afterwards one was retained another four years as shed pilot.

The Tatranská Lomnica branch became a busier line than that to Podolín as it serves one of Slovakia's most important holiday centres. Trains from Poprad now start at the Poprad-Tatry station, which is more central and is also the starting point for the electric railway into the mountains, but they still call at Poprad-Spišská Sobota.

The Štrba - Štrbské Pleso Rack Railway

There have been two lines between Štrba and Štrbské Pleso. The original one was opened in 1896 to carry tourists up from the KBD main line at Štrba (Hung. Csorba) to the mountain resort at Štrbské Pleso (Hung. Csorbato) in the High Tatra mountains, while the later re-incarnation was built by the ČSD to cater for Winter Olympic traffic in 1970.

1896 - 1932.

The original line, owned by the SPD and opened on 31st July 1896, soon passed into the control of the KBD, and passed into the ČSD in 1920. It was closed on 14th August 1932 and lifted shortly after closure. From the terminus at Štrba KBD station (896m above sea level), it rose to at height of 1350m at Štrbské Pleso. At the latter, the station was located near to the TEVZ electric station on the pleso (lakeside); it was slightly lower than the electric line station, situated below a lakeside hotel.

The 4.75 km route used steam traction in the form of two rack tank locos operating on the Riggenbach rack and pinion system. These were 0-4-0RT (Bn2zt) built by Floridsdorf in 1896, similar to the Austrian Achenseebahn locos built later. Original SPD numbers were 1 & 2, ČSD U29.001/2. For passengers the line possessed four, roofed but open-sided, four-wheel coaches (nos. 1-4), and two freight wagons, built by Ganz of Hungary.

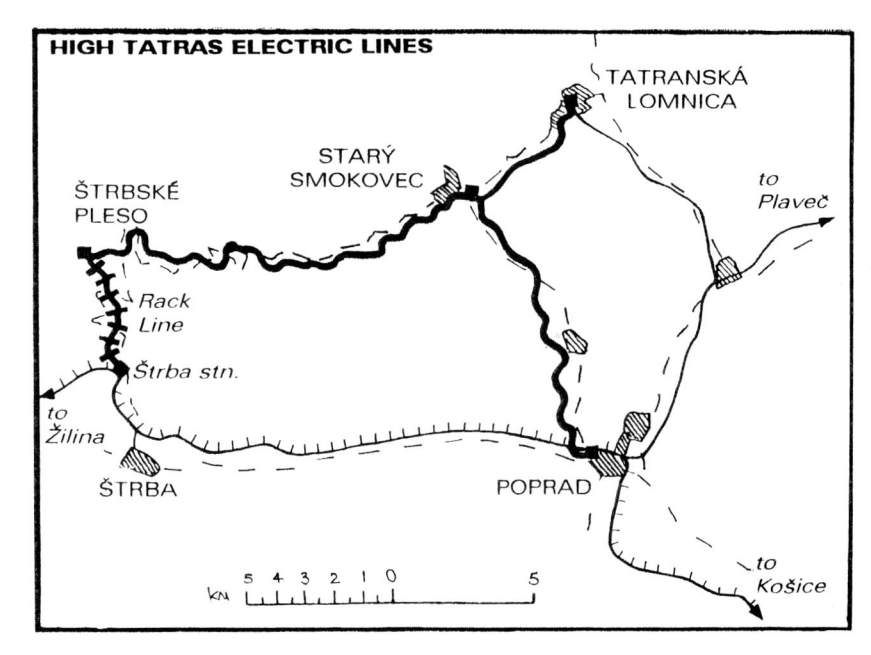

The 1969 Reconstruction.

The re-incarnation of this line occurred in the late 1960s when Czechoslovakia was preparing for the Winter Olympics traffic in 1970. From a new upper level section of Štrba station, the new metre-gauge, 1500v DC line follows much of the alignment of the original 1896 route, except at its northern end, where it was re-routed to serve the new Winter Olympics interchange at Štrbské Pleso. There is a physical connection between the rack and adhesion lines at Strbske Pleso.

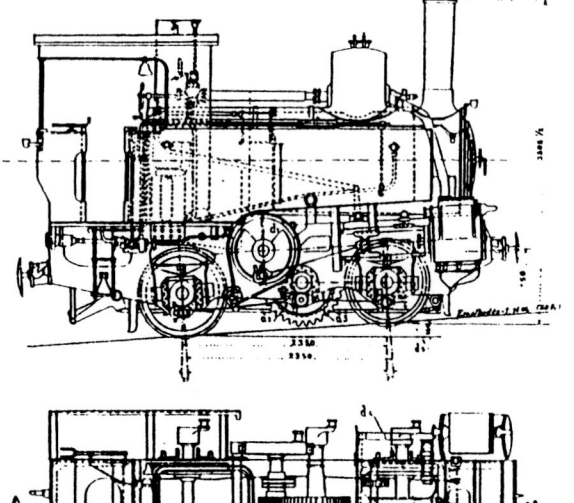

Top: The KBD timetable of the 1896 line.

Above: EMU29.001 starts the descent from Štrbské Pleso station, during August 1979.   Photo: D. James Horsford.

Left: The 1896 Floridsdorf 0-4-0RT design.

The rolling stock of the 1969 line consists of three sets of bogie two-coach electrical multiple units built by the Swiss Locomotive Works (SLM) in 1969. The motorised coaches were originally numbered EMU29.001-003, now 405.951-3, and the trailers were R29.001-003, now 905.951-3.

The Tatra Electric Railway
(Tatranská Electrická Železnice)

Known originally as the Tatranská Electrická Vicinalná dráha, it became the Tatranská Electrická Vicinalná Železnice, and ended its independence as the Tatranská Electrická Železnice, or TEŽ for short. It was taken over by the ČSD in 1952. The line uses 1500v DC.

The "TEVZ" was a metre-gauge electric network constructed to develop the emerging tourist industry in the High Tatra mountains. It linked the mountain resorts of Štrbské Pleso, Starý Smokovec and Tatranská Lomnica with the main line at Poprad. The first section of route to open was the 12.8km section between Poprad and Starý Smokovec, on 17th December 1908. The 6km branch eastwards to Tatranská Lomnica followed next, on 16th December 1911, while the final section, the 6.6 km westward route from Starý Smokovec to Štrbské Pleso opened on 13th August 1912. The total network length is 34 kms, rising from 670 m above sea level in Poprad to 1,350 m at Štrbské Pleso.

The line's alignment has altered over the years. The first change occurred in 1970 for the Winter Olympics at Štrbské Pleso. The original line was routed to a terminus along the lakeside (the pleso), but this was altered to serve the new hotel and shopping complex at the new parking/bus and train interchange built to cater for the increased traffic.

Other routing changes were made at Poprad. Until the late 1960s, the line commenced outside the main line station, on its south side, with street running over the main line to head north west through the suburbs, past the depot and out into the countryside. Subsequently, when the new Poprad station was built, the line was rerouted again, and now exits at Poprad on another new alignment, north towards the Tatra mountains.

The original architecture of the line was noteworthy, and many of the original stations remain to this day. Built in an Alpine style, the cream with brown timber framed stations blend in well with the area. The line's upper sections in the foothills of the Tatras are just as beautiful many of the Swiss metre-gauge routes, and cost far less to travel on! A trip to the various mountain resorts along this network is highly recommended.

Rolling stock:

Electrically-operated from its outset, the line was equipped initially with Hungarian-built traction.

ČSD Nos.	Year	Type	Builder	New nos.
EMU25.001	1912	4-wh	Ganz	
EMU26.001	1912	4-wh	Ganz †	
EMU28.001		4-wh		
EMU48.001-3	1912	bogie	Ganz	
EMU49.001	1931	bogie	Tatra (Smíchov)	
EMU49.002-6	1954-56	bogie	Tatra (Smíchov)	
EMU89.001	1964	8-axle*	ČKD-Tatra (Smíchov)	420.951
EMU89.002-18	1967-70	8-axle*	ČKD-Tatra (Smíchov)	420.952-68

*three-section, eight-axle articulated
†preserved and serviceable

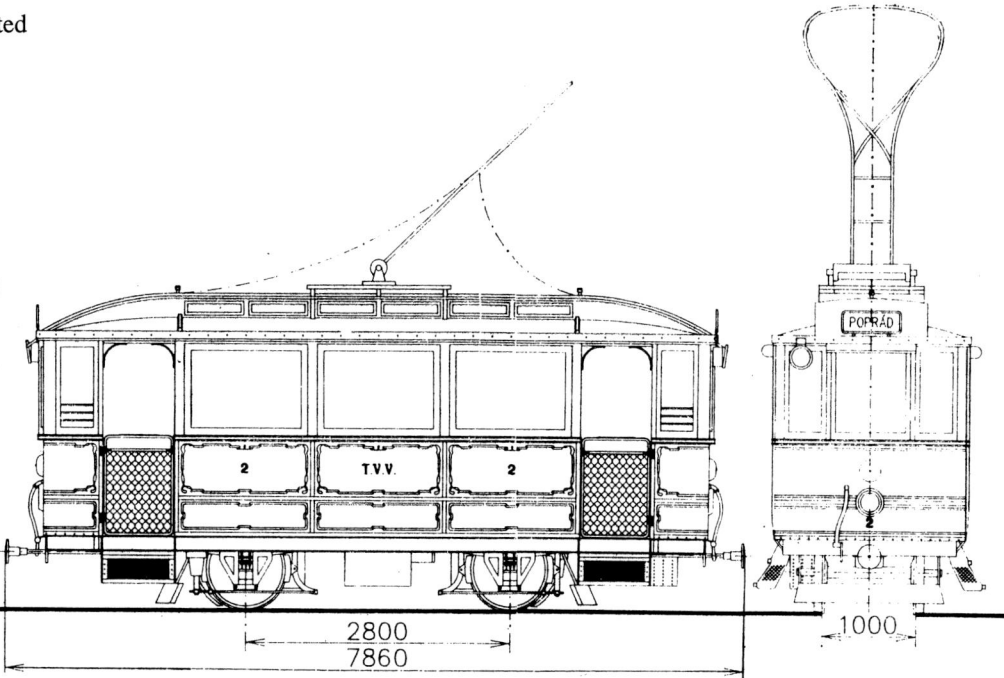

*One of the electric passenger cars built by Ganz for the opening of the line in 1908.
Drawing by Zdeněk Maruna.*

Although withdrawn at least ten years earlier, EMU49.001 was still present at Starý Smokovec in 1979, possibly as a candidate for preservation.
Photo: D. James Horsford.

The ČSD converted one of the T211.0 4-wheel shunters to metre gauge, for use on the Tatra lines' maintenance trains. In June 1991 it was still carrying its TU29.2001 identity, with the new number added below, 701.951-6.
Photo: L.I. archives.

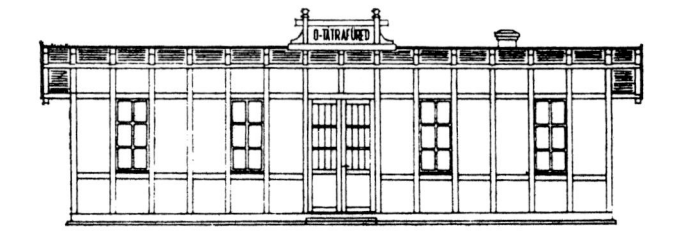

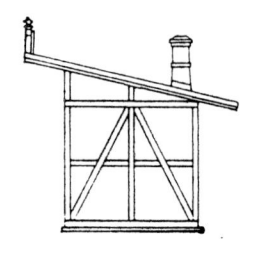

Front and side views of the 1908 station building at Smokovec.
Drawing by Zdeněk Maruna.

42

Funicular Railways and Cableways

A funicular railway from Starý Smokovec to Hrebienok and two cableways on the slopes of Lomnický štít formerly operated by the ČSD have now come under control of the ŽSR. In timetables and publicity, funiculars are described as 'pozemná lanová dráha' and suspended cableways are 'visutá lanová dráha'. Colloquially either type might be referred to as the 'lanovka'.

The funicular was in existence before the Winter Olympics were held in the Tatras, but was re-built in 1970 by the Italian firm of Ceretti-Tanfani. It is metre gauge, with two large cabins, each able to carry 128 people, and rises from 1,025 to 1,250 metres above sea level over a distance of approximately two kilometres. The cable is 31.5 mm thick. The top of the mountain, Slvkovský štít, is still some way up at 2,452 metres.

The cable cars from Tatranská Lomnica on the other hand, will take passengers almost to the peak (štít) of Lomnický štít, 2,632 metres above sea level. Two cableways start from Tatranská Lomnica, the larger capacity one just going as far as Skalnaté Pleso, (1,222 m). This has 108 cabins for four people, carried from 903 m up to 1,772 m over a distance of 3.7 kilometres. It is the newest of the cableways, operational since 1995.

The smaller capacity cableway is in two parts. The lower section carries two cabins, each for 30 people, over a distance of 4 km from Tatranská Lomnica to Skalatné Pleso, and dates from 1973. The 1.9 km long higher section has one cabin for 15 people, and was built by Van Roll of Switzerland in 1988. Two carrying cables 33 mm in diameter support the cabins, and the haulage cable is 26.5 mm thick.

CZECHOSLOVAKIAN STATE RAILWAYS - ČESKOSLOVENSKÉ STÁTNÍ DRÁHY

After independence, on 28th October 1918, the state-owned railways within the territory of the new nation were amalgamated into the ČSD. Railway building continued during the ČSD era, mainly to complete projects already started and to link up individual branches to create through routes for the network.

The first such construction finished off the line from Uzghorod to Bánovce nad Ondavou, which had been opened as far as Vojany prior to the First World War. In view of the instability of the region immediately after the conflict, this was regarded as a priority, particularly as there was some risk of losing the Čop route back to Hungary, which would have cut Sub-Carpthian Russia off the ČSD system. The alternative route to Uzghorod was open throughout from 20th October 1921.

On 15th January 1925 a line was opened through the hills from Zvolen southwards to Krupina, where it met the terminus of a branch from Šahy. This quiet secondary route was destined to see action involving the partisan armoured trains during the 1938-45 war, but today sees little more dramatic than a sparse railcar service and some freight workings.

The first train from Vojany to Bánovce was hauled by 254.401, a KBD 4-4-0 corresponding to MÁV class 220.
Photo: L.I. archives.

During the late 1920s a route was being laid from Veselí nad Moravou over the Biele Karpaty hills to Nové Mesto nad Váhom, twisting and turning most of the way on the Slovak side. It was opened as far as Myjava, today's Slovak customs point, on 8th December 1927 and the rest of the way to Nové Mesto on 1st September 1929. The first station on Slovak territory is Vrbovce zastávka, an unmanned halt at the western end of the summit tunnel. In theory, ŽSR services from Nové Mesto terminate at Myjava, and the trains over the border to the ČD customs point at Javorník nad Veličkou are operated separately, even if they do depart ten minutes after arrival using the same stock!

Another highly scenic line was built, connecting Handlová, terminus of the former MÁV branch through Prievidza, with Horná Štubňa. More tunnelling was required, through about two kilometres of hill to reach the valley of the river Turiec, and again at the junction between Horná Štubňa station and halt. Here the Handlová line, descending, crosses over the Horná Štubňa line and dives into a curved tunnel to come out on the same level for the junction. This new ČSD section was opened on 20th December 1931, and even today the 38 kms from Horná Štubňa to Prievidza, with six intermediate stops, takes over an hour by railcar - an overall average speed below 25 mph.

Perhaps the most difficult, most scenic, and certainly the most extensive railway construction project undertaken by the ČSD in the 1930s was the connecting of Červená Skala with Gelnica, creating the Zvolen - Margecany route.

Progress took time and openings took place in stages, starting initially from the western end. The first six kilometres from Červená Skala to Telgárt were in operation from 1st October 1933, then work started on the section that includes the spiral above Telgárt Penzión. References may be found in other sources to Svermovo Penzión, as it was known during the Communist era, named after a politician who is now out of favour.

Part of the Telgárt spiral is in a tunnel beyond the station, and after passing over a curved viaduct, the line plunges through another two tunnels as it gains height. The highest main line station in Slovakia, Vernar, situated 930 metres above sea level, is reached shortly after the tunnels, by which time the railway has climbed over a watershed passing from the valley of the Hron to the Hnilec, a tributary of the Hornád and Tisza. Dobšinská L'adová Jaskyňa, (now in the Slovenský Raj National Park) was reached in 1934, and the line this far was opened on 28th September.

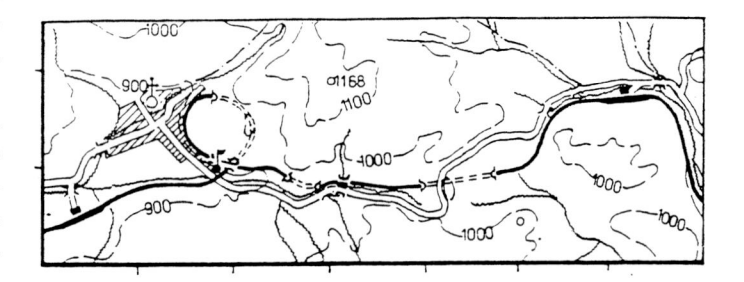

Construction continued eastwards through the 'Slovakian Paradise' to Mlynky, involving more tunnelling before the lakeside mountain resort of Dobšinská Maša was passed. Trains on this section started running on 3rd December 1935. At the same time as the line to Mlynky was being built, work was also in progress from the eastern end, converting part of the metre gauge Gelnica - Smolník line to standard gauge. Only the part of the line from Gelnica to Mníšek nad Hnilcom was reconstructed, and the rest of the line to Smolník remained in use as metre gauge. The converted section came into service just before Christmas 1935, on 22nd December.

At Prakovce, half way along the converted Gelnica to Mníšek nad Hnilcom line, 556.036 hauls an LCGB special train on September 24th 1992.

Photo: John Scrace.

Thus far, after nearly three years, only just over half the track needed to complete the Zvolen - Margecany route had been laid, reflecting the nature of the terrain, however, in about seven months the rest was ready, and through running was possible from 26th July 1936.

One of the popular excursions over the ŽSR is 'doing' the Zvolen - Margecany line, table 170 in the 'Cestovný Poriadok'. This is a long day's riding, and probably only possible in a day by travelling out and back on the 'Horehronec' express. It can be done from Bratislava, departing around 6 a.m. and arriving back at 11 p.m., with an early afternoon lay-over of about an hour and a half at Margecany. Indeed before the ČSD was split it was possible to travel overnight on a through coach from Prague, but now sleeping cars travelling from the ČD use the ex-KBD route.

Few passenger trains actually travel the whole distance of table 170, as even now it is operated virtually as two branches from either end with an intermediate section between Brezno and Červená Skala - and there can be significant lengths of time between some connections.

Tractive power on the line was a mixture of ex-MÁV and ČSD types until the arrival of the elegant 475.0 class 4-8-2s. These mixed traffic locomotives with daylight between their wheels and boiler, took command of passenger services until displaced by the 'Frowning' class T478.1 diesels. Most passenger trains now are in the hands of railcars, although normally the 'Horehronec' will be headed by one of the variants of the 'Goggles' class Bo-Bo.

Freights were handled for many years by the ČSD 534.0 class 2-10-0s, the combination of light axle load and high haulage capacity being ideally suited to what was essentially an extended mountain branch line. In later years heavier locos were in use, including the 556.0 2-10-0s and the orange T678.0 'Pomeranč' diesels (775), but none were heavier or worse for the track than the 116-tonne Russian-built class T679.1 'Sergei' Co-Cos!

T679.021 represents the passenger version of the 'Pomeranč' at Brezno on a summer evening in 1974. The two types were built 1961-65 by ČKD, and are of an older generation of diesels. The last of the T679.0s (as class 776) were withdrawn in 1997, but a couple have been preserved.
Photo: D. James Horsford.

A couple of years after the completion of the Zvolen - Margecany line a new route was built from the Slovak town of Púchov to Vsetin in Moravia. The opening took place on 2nd May 1937, and services were electrified from 12th September 1960. By creating a new route to Olomouc it was possible to avoid the punishing gradients of the Jablunka pass and the congested industrial area of Ostrava. Not many local trains now run on the 1937 route, but it carries a number of the main expresses run between the Czech and Slovak Republics, and a heavy tonnage of freight passes through the border points of Strelenka (ŽSR) and Horní Lideč (ČD).

The last new building undertaken by the ČSD before the 1938-45 war was a branch line from Zlaté Moravce to Zbehy opened on 16th May 1938. It's a meandering line in rolling countryside serving no apparent major purpose, other than perhaps providing a short cut from Zlaté Moravce to Nitra, or Leopoldov. For many years the ČSD has operated this line plus the branches from Leopoldov to Zbehy and Zlaté Moravce to Kozárovce as a single route, integrated with connections to and from Nitra. Trains are normally made up of class 810 railcars and trailers, the M152.0 and Baafx of ČSD origin.

As Slovakia did not generally suffer the sort of fighting and bombing that other countries did until near the end of the Second World War, it was possible for railway building to continue. Ironically the first of the two lines laid by the 1938-45 Slovenské Železnice was one of those to see wartime action, as described in the section on the armoured trains of the SNP partisans.

The line in question is a branch north-west from Banská Bystrica that joins up with the line to Vrútky at Horná Štubňa. The route diverges from the Margecany line and does a U-turn round the eastern edge of the town before plunging into the first of twenty-two tunnels in thirty-nine kilometres. Your author, travelling on an overnight express from Zvolen to Prague, tried to count the tunnels by the changing sound of the rails, but this proved more effective than counting sheep - I must have been asleep before Uľanka was reached!

From Uľanka to Harmanec jaskyňa is approximately 7 km as the crow flies, but the railway takes 14 km, during the course of which it twice goes into a tunnel only to re-emerge coming out of the other end in the opposite direction. The first time is after crossing the Starohorský Potok (potok = stream), and the second is when following the upper waters of the river Bystrica between Dolní Harmanec and Harmanec jaskyňa (jaskyňa = cave, for which this area is noted). The second of these two particular tunnels contains a horseshoe curve entirely within the mountainside.

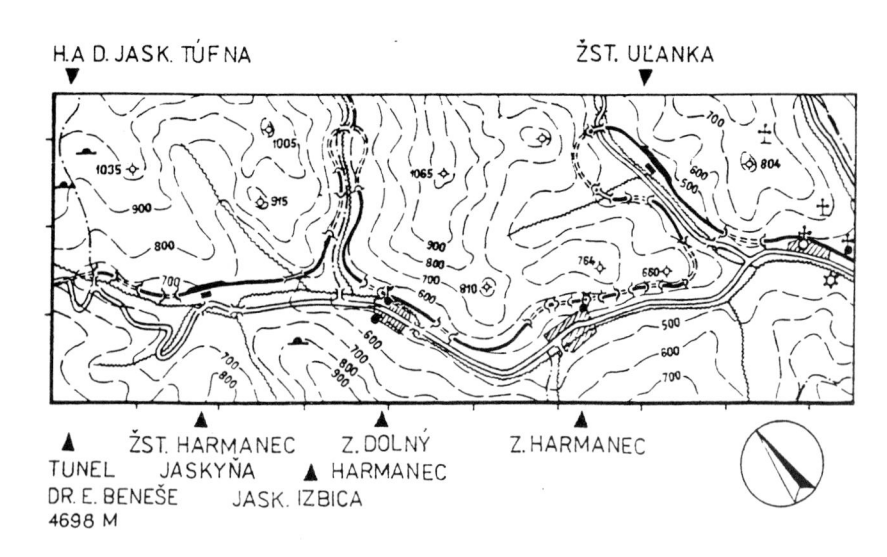

'Goggles' class 754.071-9 stands at the head of train number 21207, an afternoon all-stops from Vrútky to Banská Bystrica, seen at Harmanec jaskyňa station in October 1997.
Photo: ing. Juraj Greguš.

Another line was built during the war, towards the eastern end of the country connecting Kapušany pri Prešove with Strážske by way of Vranov nad Topľou. Parts of southern Slovakia had been seized by Hungary in November 1938, including Košice and the southern ends of the lines to Vranov and Medzilaborce, both of which thus became cut off from the rest of the Slovenské Železnice. The new railway re-established a means of transport through to the eastern end of Poland.

By Slovak standards the route was not a difficult one, following the valley of the river Topľa for the greater part of its distance. At the Strážske end, after the one tunnel on the line, the junction with the Medzilaborce line was built south of the station as a triangle, enabling trains to proceed north or southbound without delay. The railway was opened on 5th September 1943, operating on a Prešov - Strážske - Humenné timetable as these are the two more important junction towns beyond either end.

It was a few years before any more railways were constructed as the necessity in the latter half of the '40s was the rebuilding of war-damaged infrastructure and worn-out rolling stock - as with most of the rest of Europe. The only major new work undertaken in the 1940s was the gauge conversion of the Hronská Dúbrava - Banská Štiavnica line, as described in the narrow gauge section.

The Hungarian influence on motive power was still evident on 8th September 1969 when 344.450 was photographed at Prešov depot. Next to it is a 475.0 or 498.0, judging by the 935.0 series tender, and inside the shed is a class 464.0 tank loco. Photo: Jan Koutný.

The next new line built was the branch to the village of Malé Straciny, something of a curiosity, as it is actually a branch off a Hungarian line running back into Slovakia. When the line was planned, relations between Czechoslovakia and Hungary must have improved, presumably under the mutual comradeship of Communism, for services were to run between Lučenec and through Hungary to Malé Straciny, as indeed they did from 12th September 1951. Once trains were out of Czechoslovakia and onto Hungarian territory, they ran non-stop until back in Czechoslovakia, avoiding customs formalities. Since the end of Communism and the break-up of the ČSD, however, the service beyond the first border station of Kalonda has been suspended. Actually it's not clear quite why the ČSD went to the trouble and complication of building this minor branch in the first place, but even more surprising is that it was another twenty-seven years before they extended it three kilometres to Velké Krtíš, the only town of any significance nearby, and a more obvious terminal point. Citizens of Velké Krtíš first gained their own train service on 30th May 1978.

Going back to our chronological sequence, 23rd January 1955 to be exact, a section of railway with a more obvious benefit was brought into use. This was the 31 km from Rožňava to Turňa nad Bodvou, laid to form a connection from Zvolen and the branches in the south of the country to Košice. Turňa nad Bodvou was the border point for a former Hungarian North Eastern Railway line crossing into Slovakia, though this has been closed in recent years, at least for passenger traffic, if not freight as well.

Although not a route that carries a large volume of traffic, it does see a few named expresses working between Košice and Bratislava or Budapest, in addition to which are a few stopping trains, mainly timed for working peoples' use. For the enthusiast travelling from Bratislava to Košice or vice versa the route provides a useable alternative to the electrified main line through Žilina and the Tatras. It is about the same length at around 440 kilometres and the journey takes about an hour longer, but diesel traction takes over from electric beyond Zvolen.

The last section of standard gauge track laid in the Tatras was a connection from Plaveč to Podolínec, enabling a more direct connection from the PKP at Nowy Sacz to Poprad. The Polish line to Nowy Sacz is electrified, and the wires continue into Slovakia, through Orlov as far as Plaveč. It is questionable as to how much steam traction the section to Podolínec has seen, as railcars were in use in the Tatras long before it was built, and diesels were available for freight. Mid-way along the route is the old town of Stará L'ubovňa, with a ruined castle and an open-air museum of traditional Slovak architecture of the Špis region.

In the summer of 1997 floods devastated northern Moravia and closed the lines to Poland west of the Tatras. As a result the line from Poprad to Orlov saw an increased quantity of trains as passenger services and freights alike were diverted hundreds of kilometres to avoid wash-outs.

A 5' ČSD gauge line from the Ukraine runs well into Slovakia alongside the standard gauge from Uzghorod to the VSZ steelworks at Haniska, avoiding the need to either change bogies at the border or to use the giant freight transhipment centre just inside the Ukraine. It was mainly built along the existing route to Bánovce nad Ondavou, but turns away at Trebišov to meet the Čierna nad Tisou - Košice line at Kalša, and again parallels the existing track to a point just south of Košice. The standard gauge from Bánovce eastwards was terminated at Vel'ké Kapušany when the Russian gauge was built on the same trackbed beyond the town, but has recently been reinstated into Uzghorod for freight. Services over the new broad gauge line were inaugurated on Mayday 1966.

The last ČSD line to be built in Slovakia was a standard gauge section a few kilometres long following the broad gauge track between Trebišov and Kalša. It was opened on 7th November 1985, and in addition to freight trains, sees several expresses bound for Humenné, for which it makes a short-cut avoiding Michal'any. Very few stopping trains travel over the new line.

At the time of writing the newest line in Slovakia is the relaid crossing over the border from the rebuilt Bratislava-Petržalka station to another relaid section in Austria that connects through to Vienna. This is due to be officially inaugurated with great 'pomp and circumstance' a few weeks after publication, on August 20th 1998, 150 years after the arrival of the first steam-hauled train into Bratislava.

The ČSD's two big blue three-cylinder 4-8-2 express classes photographed by A.E. Durrant:

Left: The ČSD's first postwar express locomotives were the handsome class 498.0. At Nové Zámky on 21st October 1958 498.026 heads an express train towards the Hungarian border, whilst nobody takes exception to my photography. Note allocation to the Bratislavská Dráha, or railway marked on the buffer beam.

Below: First of the class, no. 498.101, calls at Nové Zámky whilst hauling a westbound ČSD express on the same day.

48

ČSD NARROW GAUGE LINES

Ružomberok station, March 1997. Photo: Paul Catchpole.

Ružomberok - Korytnica   760 mm gauge.

After construction of the standard gauge line from Kral'ovany to Suchá Hora, the citizens of Ružomberok set their hopes on another line which would provide a route to Banská Bystrica without having to go the long way round on the Košice-Bohumín Railway. A further benefit from such a line would be a means of transport for wood from the Korytnica and Revúce valleys, used for paper and cellulose production in Ružomberok. Moving the timber by road was expensive, and attempts to float the logs down the rivers to economise had evidently not proved satisfactory.

A Ružomberok - Korytnica Railway company was set up in 1906 with backing from the local council, and raised sufficient funds for building to commence. The Ministry of Trade tendered for construction of the line and assent was granted on 12th December 1906. Ružomberok council then withdrew financial support on the grounds that all costs were being borne by those in the 'south' - by which they probably meant Bratislava or Budapest rather than the southern end of the line. The railway company engaged in a legal battle with the council, which it won in 1910.

Construction, undertaken by the firm of Mandel and Reverx, started in 1907, using a gauge of 760 mm. The line was laid along the valley of the rivers Revúca and Korytnica through Biely Potok (meaning White Stream), and Liptovská Osada to Korytnica. Korytnica itself is a small town with a spa at the nearby village of Korytnica kúpele, while Liptovská Osada is a village below the town and skiing centre of Liptovská Lúžna.

Traffic over the 23.5 km line commenced on 5th June 1908, then in May 1910 a subsidy was received for construction of spurs to the Hungarian Pulping and Cellulose works in Biely Potok. The question of extending to Banská Bystrica was raised by the Ružomberok council, with the addition of a proposal for

The Korytnica 0-8-0T design, drawn by Josef Janata.

RUŽOMBEROK - KORYNICA-KÚPELE

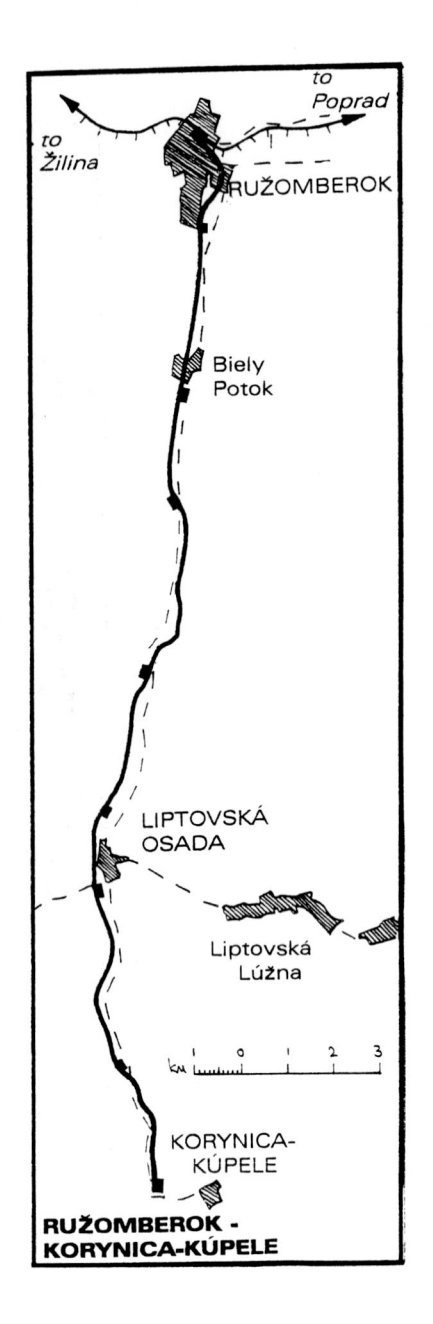

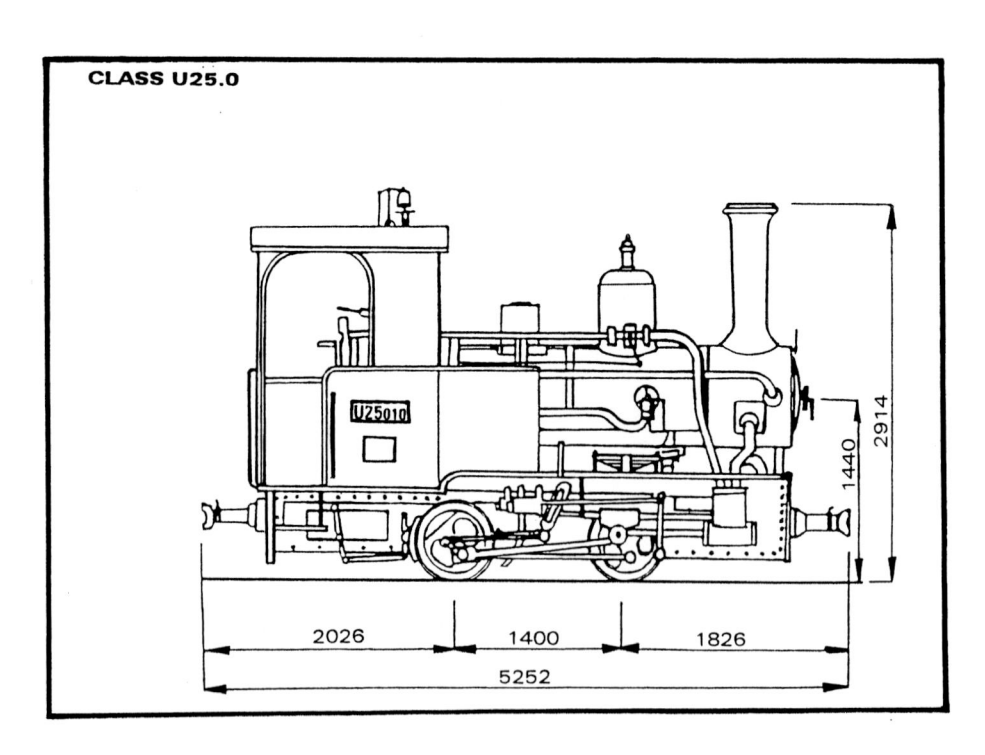

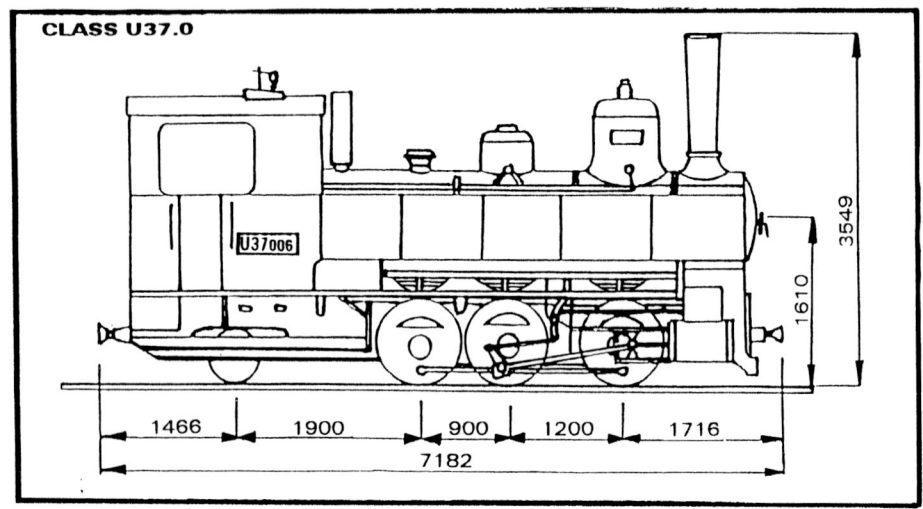

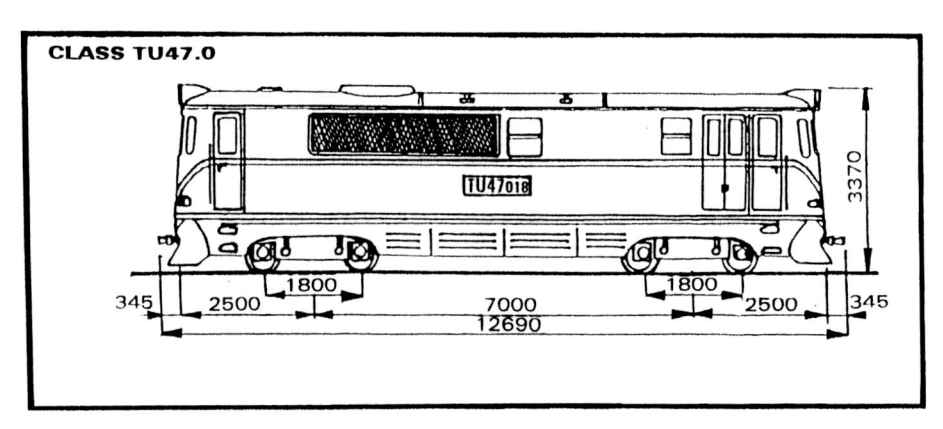

CLASS U25.0

CLASS U37.0

CLASS TU47.0

conversion to standard gauge, but the necessary financial resources were not forthcoming, so nothing happened. In 1919 the matter was pursued again through the legal system. If this action had succeeded it would have involved building twelve tunnels, one of them 2,050 metres long. The cost would have been very high, but again nothing came of it.

Other plans were made for through routes from Hungary to Poland via Štúrovo, Zvolen and Ružomberok on alignments which would have enabled trains of 150 axles to be hauled by a

After closure of the line to Korytnica in 1974 the newer rolling stock was re-allocated to the Jindřichův Hradec narrow gauge system and U37.006 was plinthed in the small park beside Rožumberok station.
Photo: D. James Horsford.

single locomotive, a considerable saving on existing operations, however, at the end of the day other routes had been in operation for some years and the investment was not considered to be worth while by the ČSD.

When the line opened it employed rolling stock built by Ganz and a trio of Budapest locomotive factory 0-8-0T built in 1908 (works numbers 1993-1995). These were essentially a 'stretched' version of the MÁV class 490 (ČSD U.45.0), and were similarly equipped with Klein-Lindner axles to allow tight curves to be negotiated. They were such excellent locomotives that during the First World War the Austro-Hungarian army took them to Serbia for use on supply lines, but unfortunately they got left in Italy and never came back. An 0-6-0T was borrowed from a forestry line, however, the boiler had expired by 1922.

Following this motive power crisis at least one of the U25.0 class 0-4-0T was obtained, but these were a rather small substitute for the former locos, and an MÁV type 490 0-8-0 was obtained from the army, numbered initially U46.001, but re-numbered in 1927 to U45.002 as another loco of the same type existed on the Beregovo system in Sub-Carpathian Russia. In 1928/29 two Austrian U class 0-6-2T from the Třemešná ve Slezsku - Osoblaha line that had been taken into PKP stock during the 1914-18 war were returned to the ČSD and one of these, U37.011, was allocated to Ružomberok in 1931. Sister loco U37.006 was also transferred in 1931, followed at some later time by U37.003, both having become surplus to requirements with the closure of the Moravský Beroun - Dvorce line. Diesel traction arrived in 1958 and U37.003/011 were taken out of service in 1959. U37.006 carried on till 1960, but instead of being scrapped was plinthed in front of Ružomberok station.

Two diesel locomotives took over from the three U class, namely TU 47.018 and TU 47.021. The TU 47.0 were the first standard ČSD diesel class, all built by ČKD in Prague from 1954 on, and employed on the various narrow gauge lines of the ČSD. Some are still in action today on the Czech lines centred on Jindřichův Hradec, now renumbered by the ČD as class 705. Passenger rolling stock was also renewed with the introduction of bogie coaches of type Balm/u.

The line to Korytnica never was converted to standard gauge or extended, and in fact it was closed in 1974 following a period of economic decline. The last passenger train ran on 28th September 1974, composed of TU 47.018 hauling Balm/u coaches 662 and 669.

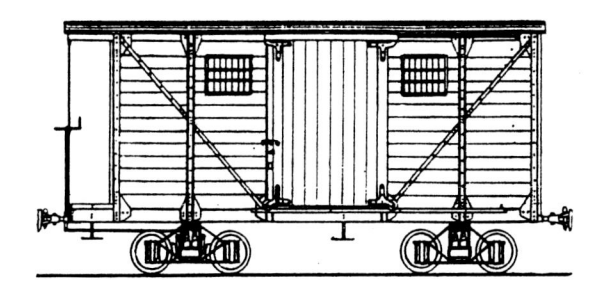

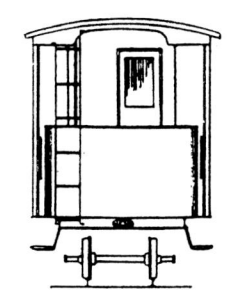

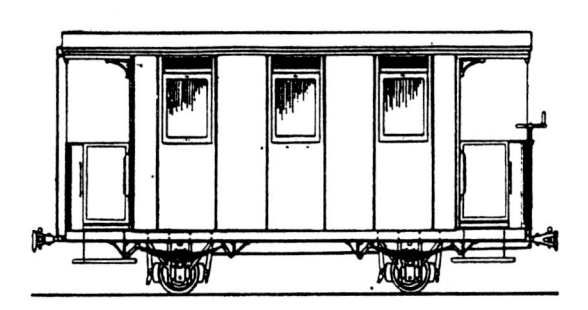

Examples of the original Rožumberok - Korytnice rolling stock.

51

Trenčianska Teplá - Trenčianske Teplice   760 mm gauge

Constructed to promote tourism, this 5.9 km long, 760mm gauge, electric roadside tramway links the spa town of Trenčianska Teplice with the main Bratislava - Žilina railway line at Trenčianska Teplá. Originally known in Hungarian as the Holak-Trencsentepliczi Villamos Vasút" (Teplá-Trenčianské Teplice Electric Railway), the line opened to electric traction (750v DC) on 27th July 1909. It was originally operated by three small electric trams, nos.1-3, along with passenger trailers 14 and 15, closed freight van no.51 and open wagon no.101. A fourth tram was added to the fleet in 1911, and the line's voltage was increased to 950v DC in 1942.

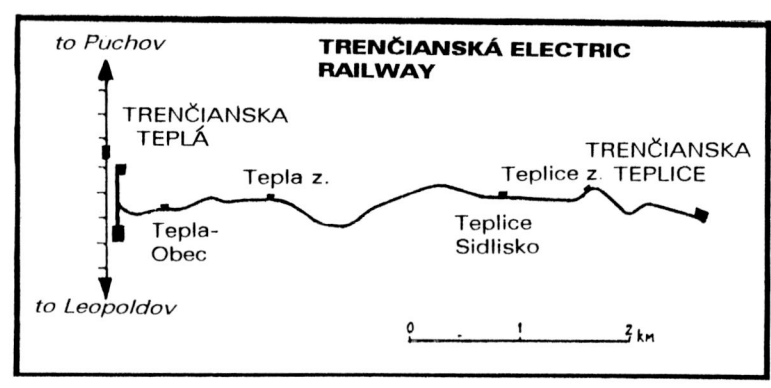

The original four cars operated the whole service until 1951, when the three bogie cars, (M46.001-3), were built by Studénka. Additionally, three trailers were built, Calm/u 500-2., one (500) by Studénka in 1951 and the other two by Česká Lípa in 1954. The original cars were withdrawn in 1966, with EMU24.001 being preserved. In 1983, the three 1951 cars and trailers were rebuilt with new bodies by DP Ostrava.

The depot is located at Trenčianska Teplá.

Rolling stock:

Nos.	Year	Type	Seats	Builder	New nos.
EMU24.001-3	1909	4-wh	24	Gyor	
EMU24.004	1911	4-wh	?	Ganz	
EMU46.001-3	1951	bogie	49*	Tatra(Studénka)	411.901-3
Balm/u 649**	1951	bogie trailer		Tatra (Studénka)	?
Balm/u 650/1**	1954	bogie trailer		Česká Lípa	911.901/2

*originally 46 seats.   **Originally Calm/u 500-3.

Užhorod - Antalovce 760 mm gauge (became Uzgorod - Antonovka, Ukraine)

This 760 mm gauge line was built during the First World War from Ungvar (Cz. Uzhorod), off the main Ung Valley, up to the area around Antoloc, 36 kms away, and served the forestry section of the SZD until closure during the 1960s or 1970s. Its inclusion here is merited by it having been operated by ČSD using locomotives which also worked in Slovakia. Now a Ukrainian regional centre, Uzgorod is just over the frontier from Slovakia, and used standard Austro-Hungarian motive power until replacement by Czech and Soviet diesels in the 1950s.

The earliest locos on the line became ČSD class U25.0, but their exact identity is unknown. They were withdrawn in 1937. Also in 1937 railcars M11.003/4, originally built for the Borza Valley Railway in Ruthenia were transferred to this line. They were taken into MÁV stock when Hungary annexed the area in 1939, and fell into USSR territory after 1945. In addition to other locomotives listed below, U37.011 also worked briefly on this railway (see Rožumberok - Korytnica). The other two U37.0 were transferred between 1927-31.

industry of the area. In 1921, it was taken over by ČSD. The line continued a quiet existence, surviving two world wars, several changes of nationality, and finally ended up as a narrow-gauge

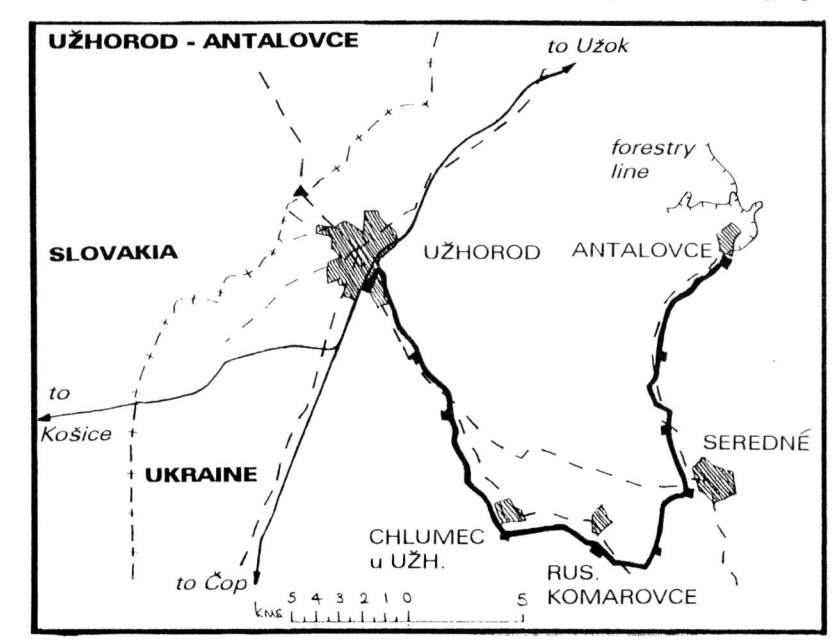

Rolling stock:
U25.001-10	1917	0-4-0T Bm2t	Orenstein & Koppel
U37.001	1897	0-6-2T C1'm2t	Krauss (Linz) 3638
U37.005	1906	0-6-2T C1'm2t	Erste Bohm.- Mar. 175
U37.010	1898	0-6-2T C1'm2t	Krauss (Linz) 3817
M11.003/4	1928	Railcar	Tatra Koprvnice*

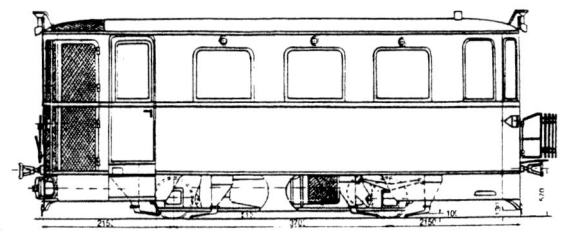

U37.001 from Jindřichův Hradec in 1927; to MÁV 1938, no.394.001, later 395.101, scrapped in Hungary 1963.
U37.005 from Teresva in 1930; to MAV 1938, no.394.002, later 395.102, to USSR 1945, fate unknown.
U37.010 from Jindrichuv Hradec in 1931; to MAV 1938, no 394.003, later 395.103, to USSR 1945, fate unknown.

A Russian-built TU2.044 diesel takes an LCGB 'special' for a trip along the Uzgorod - Antonovka line, passing a stork's nest on it's journey. Photo: D. Trevor Rowe.

NARROW GAUGE FORESTRY RAILWAYS

Ex-Oščadnica - Zákamenné Forest Railway 0-8-0T no. 1 and guard's van, at Oščadnica on 15th May 1971. Photo: Anon. L.I. archives.

Kysuce - Orava Forest Railway, Vychylovka

In 1926 two existing forestry systems were connected by a new line creating a network of 110 km. The first of the existing systems was from beside the KBD at Oščadnica to Vychylovka and the Chmura valley, and the other along the river Biela Orava from Lokča to Oravská Lesná. The new railway was engineered through difficult terrain, and required several reversals to gain height. It is this section between Vychylovka and Tanečník that has been preserved within the context of the open-air skansen 'Muzeum Kysucké Dediny' at Vychylovka. The railway system was cut short to Zákamenné from 1968, and finally closed in its entirety officially on 31st December 1971, but the central section was retained for the museum with the aid of a supporters group. The museum as a whole consists of a collection of buildings showing folk architechture and the older way of life in the area, with the added attraction of a forest railway operating a summer passenger service with steam power.

Locomotives not in use are kept under cover, but normally on display, all 0-8-0Ts, including 'Gontkulák' (ČKD 1441/1928), no. 154 (Krauss-Maffei 15791/1939), no. 1 (Budapest 4281/1916), and no.5 (Henschel 20615/1926). The operational locomotives at the time of writing are normally U45.903, which is an ex-Liptovsky Hrádok MÁV 490 type 0-8-0 (Budapest 4280/1916), and ex-Hronec forestry line 0-6-0T no. U34.901 (Budapest 2282/09).

54

U45.903, formerly of the Povážská Lesná Železnica pushes it's single coach train up a reversal with the aid of U34.903 at the other end! Photo: August 1987, L.I. archives.

Povážská Lesná Železnica, Liptovský Hrádok 760 mm gauge

This 104 km long network (at its greatest extent) was constructed to 760 mm gauge to transport timber from the upper valleys of the Čierny Váh river down to the mills at Liptovský Hrádok. It was a vast system, known as the Váh Forestry Railway. Most of the motive power took the form of 0-8-0T, but a number of bogie railcars were also used in the line's later days.

Rolling stock:

No.	Year	Type	Builder
U45.901-5	1916*	0-8-0T	MAVAG*
4-199	1950	0-8-0	Škoda*
M21.003	1939	B'2'	Tatra Koprvnice
M21.006	1948	B'2'	Tatra Koprvnice
M21.008	1948	B'2'	Tatra Koprvnice
23/32	1961	B-B	RAMA
?	1943	B	Gebus

* 4-199 is preserved at Liptovský Hrádok.

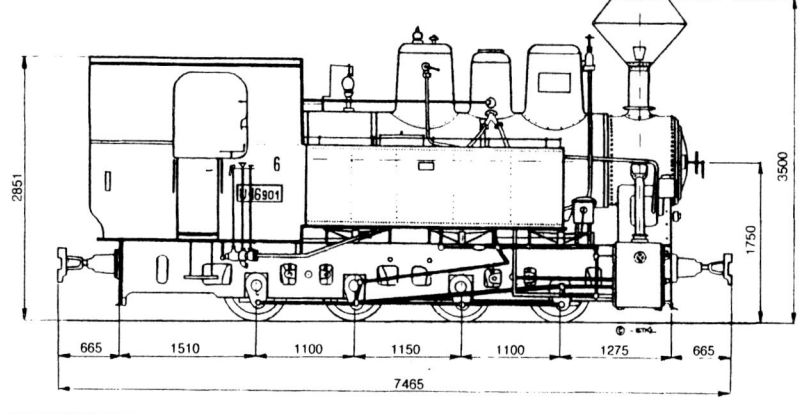

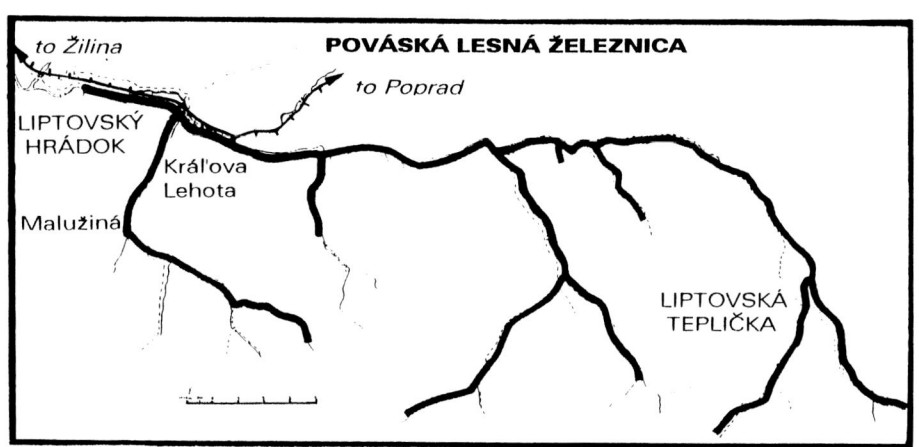

The railway ceased operation on 1st January 1973, and most of the line was abandoned. Only a small section around the mills and timber yards in Liptovský Hrádok remained in use, shunted by one of the diesel locos. All was not over then however, as in June 1973, some TV filming took place on the line, using one of the steam locos. It had been intended to operate some 15 kms of the route as a preserved steam tourist line, between Liptovksý Hrádok and Liptovská Teplička, but nothing came of the plan.

55

Hronec Forestry Railway

A full account of the Čiernohronská Železnica appeared in our earlier book 'East European Narrow Gauge', but this volume would be incomplete without some basic details of this, the leading preserved narrow gauge railway. Credit for preservation must go to the efforts of 'Strom Života', meaning 'Tree of Life', not a railway group as such, but more the equivalent of the 'Friends of the Earth' volunteer environmental organisation.

The ČHŽ is based at Hronec, but for connections from Brezno and Podbrezova on the Zvolen - Margecany main line, runs a railcar, M131.1053, which is in itself a museum-piece. Services run all year round on weekends and some holidays, and connect with the 'Horehronec' express. In keeping with the conservation aspect of the railway, bicycles can be transported on all the trains and a network of cycle tracks exists around the railway. A timetable and information for the railway can be found in the ŽSR timetable (Cestovný Poriadok), normally printed after table 170.

In addition to the steam locomotives described in EENG, the railway also has some diesel motive power, including an M21.0 railcar no. M21.008, a 'Rába' 4-wheel diesel loco, standard for Hungarian Forestry Railways, and draisine no. Š1202 which can be hired privately.

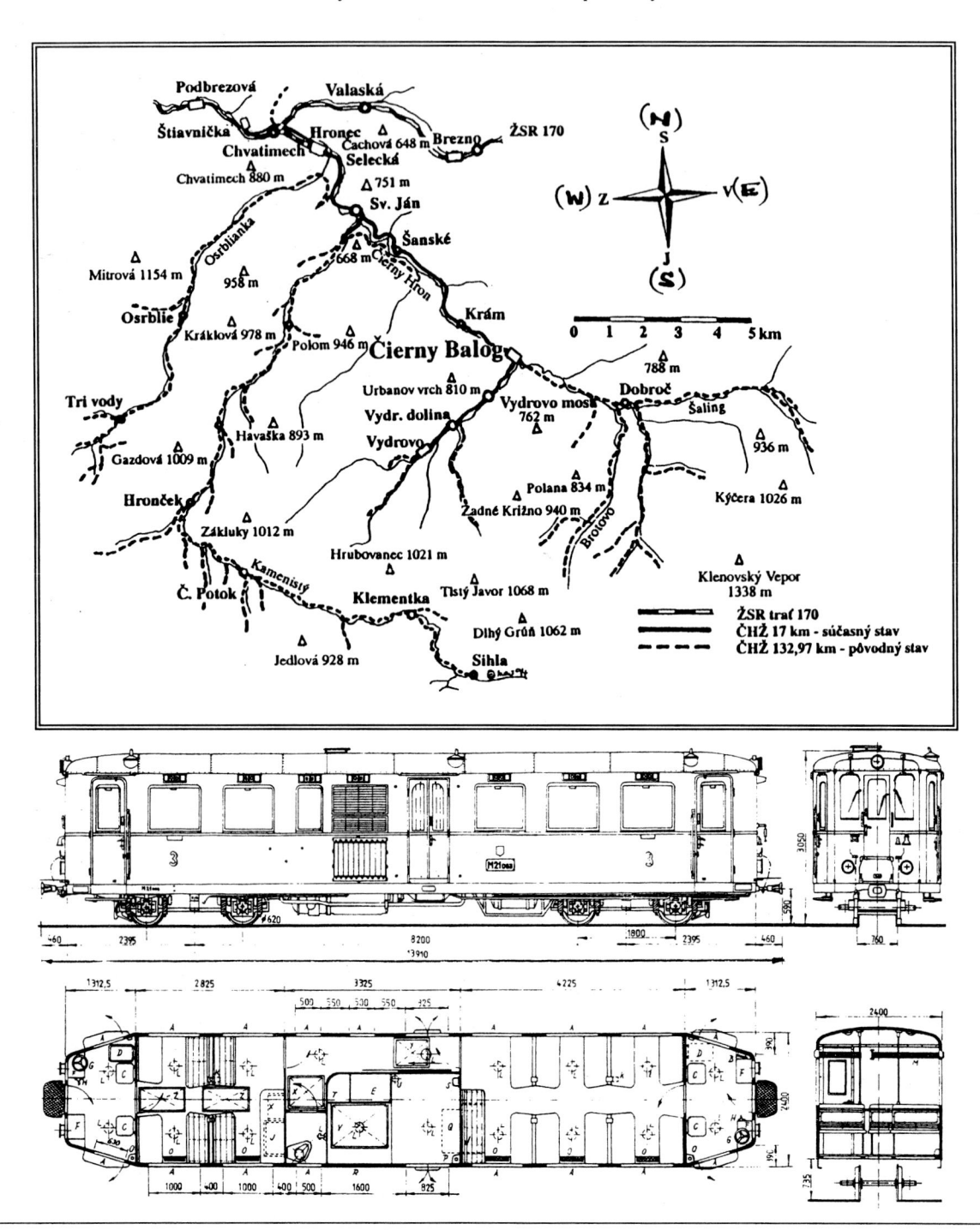

56

FORMER METRE GAUGE RAILWAYS

In addition to the Štrba - Štrbské Pleso line described in the chapter covering the railways in the Tatras, Slovakia had three other metre gauge railways, Hronská Dúbrava-Banská Štiavnica, Gelnica-Smolník and the Čermel 'young pioneer' railway operated by young people of school age. The latter is the only one still running as a metre gauge line, and as an added bonus it can also boast steam traction. The other two were both converted in whole or part to standard gauge.

U35.103 was a miniature version of the contemporary main line engines, built for the Banská Štiavnica line in 1873. In this scene from 1956 it was working on the Čermel 'Pioneer' Railway near Košice. Photo: L.I. archives.

Hronská Dúbrava - Banská Štiavnica

Banská Štiavnica and the surrounding areas have a long history of silver mining, in fact 'Banská' means 'mining'. The town and its silver were the source of wealth for the Hungarian Fugger family whose banking business was an important element in Hungary's economy. In 1762 a mining academy was opened and the town went through a boom period, so that by the end of the 18th century Banská Štiavnica was the second largest town in Slovakia.

The railway was the first narrow gauge line built by the MÁV, starting beside the main line west of Zvolen at Hronská Dúbrava, then known as Hronská Breznice. After crossing the river Hron the track made its way up into the hills, following contours as much as possible, but still involving numerous embankments and cuttings.

On 10th October 1873 the railway opened using three 0-6-0 tender engines built by G. Sigl at Wiener Neustadt, works numbers 1096-1098 of 1873. To these a fourth was added, built at Budapest works, inventory number 1197/1897. Originally MÁV class XX, they became class 387 in 1911, and were later absorbed into the ČSD who renumbered them to U35.101-104 in the 1925 re-classification.

Conversion to standard gauge took place in 1947 during the universities' summer vacation, when students and teachers were available to perform the manual labour necessary. The metre gauge was in operation up to 27th October 1947, and from 28th the standard gauge went into service. From this time forth the line has been known as the "Trat' Mladeže", in English the "Youth Railway".

The standard gauge line was not able to follow the alignment of the original trackbed all the way, due to the tight curves and nature of the landscape. A new bridge was built to cross the river Hron, and the old route ran on a lower alignment as far as Kozelník. Shortly after Kozelník station the metre gauge line went round and below today's cutting, and crossed briefly over the river in the valley before meeting up with the present-day route at Banská Belá town station. The routes again diverged as the metre gauge crossed to the west side of the valley, and remained apart until a point after Banský Studenec where there was a halt simply called 'km 19.810 zastávka'! Beyond here the same trackbed is followed, passing through a tunnel about a kilometre long before the terminus at Banská Štiavnica. The metre gauge route was 23 km in length, whereas the standard gauge is just 20 km.

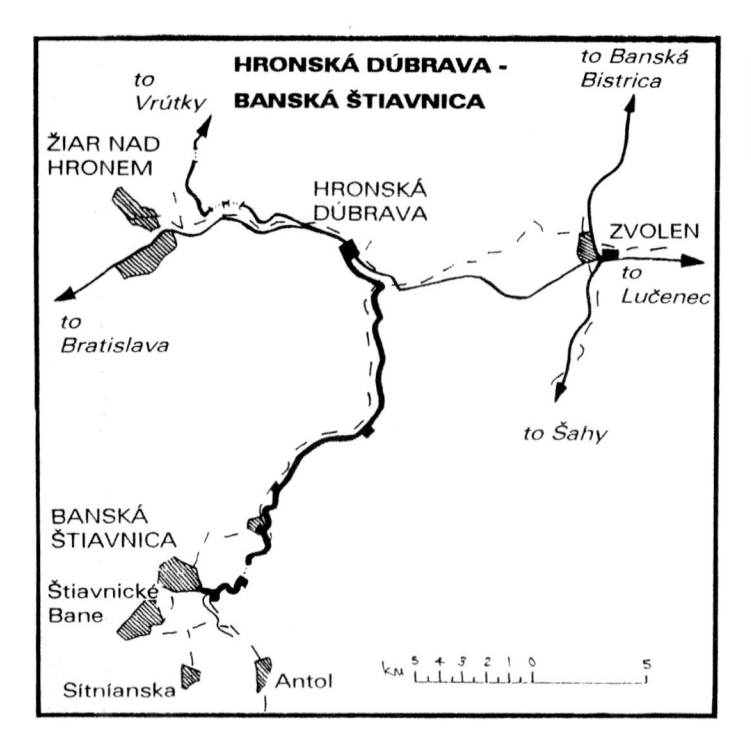

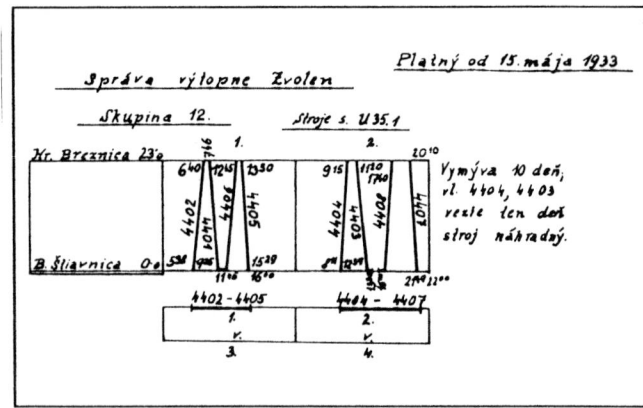

Locomotive working diagram of 1933

The original bridge over the river Hron in October 1997. Some reconstruction has taken place as the bridge has been narrowed and no longer occupies the full width of the wooden supports. The bridge now carries a footpath along the old trackbed from the south side of the river almost as far as the station.

34 p Hronská Dúbrava – Banská Štiavnica (Úzkorozchodná železnica)

								km	Čís. vlaku Trieda Riad. Bratislava Trieda	km								
...	...	6.55		6.05	13.00	17.50	...		odch. Bratislava hl. n. 31, 34 .... prích.		...	8.00	13.49	18.30		18.20		23.41
4.54		11.06		13.54	16.59	21.27			odch. Zvolen 34			4.53	7.12	11.13		15.53	17.40	22.07
2.40	...	9.06	...	11.25	14.50	17.44			odch. Martin–Vrútky 35 .... prích.			7.40	12.09	12.57		16.50	21.42	22.03
3302	3304	3306		3308	3310	3312		km	Čís. vlaku Trieda	km		3301	3303	3305		3307	3309	3311
3.	2,3.	2,3.		3.	2,3.	3.						3.	2,3.	2,3.		2,3.	2,3.	3.
...	5.20	7.20	11.31	14.12	17.40	23.25	...	0	odch. **Hronská Dúbrava** [3] ✕ .... prích.	23	...	3.40	6.36	10.22	...	13.56	17.00	18.59	...	...
...	5.43	7.43	11.54	14.35	18.03	23.49		9	Kozelník z	14		3.17	6.13	9.59		13.33	16.37	18.36
...	6.01	7.59	12.10	14.51	18.19	0.05		14	Žakýl z	9		3.03	5.59	9.44		13.19	16.23	18.22
...	6.10	8.08	12.19	15.00	18.28	0.14		17	Banská Belá z.	6		2.53	5.44	9.34		13.09	16.13	18.04
...	6.18	8.16	12.27	15.08	18.36	0.22		—	km 19,810 z	—		2.46	5.36	9.26		13.01	16.05	17.56
...	6.28	8.26	12.37	15.18	18.46	0.32		23	prích. **Banská Štiavnica** 🚂 odch.	0		2.35	5.25	9.15		12.50	15.54	17.45

Timetable for the metre gauge services in 1940.

The former metre gauge railway station at Hronská Dúbrava some time after conversion, as shown by the presence of a colour light signal on the main line. This photo was taken from the standard gauge platform opposite.
Photo: Courtesy ŽSR.

The standard gauge station as at 5th October 1997. Standing at the platform is railcar 810.535-5 and its trailer, forming the mid-morning train to Banská Štiavnica.
Photo: Paul Catchpole.

U35.101 was badly damaged during the 1938-45 war and had been scrapped before the line was converted to standard gauge. U35.102 and U35.104 were scrapped at Banská Štiavnica in 1962, having stood there since 1947, but U35.103 had a new lease of life on the Smolník line from 1949 till 1955. Along with 0-6-0T U36.004 the loco was moved to the Čermel Pioneers' Railway near Košice, but they were both scrapped in an economy drive, and U35.103's boiler suffered the awful fate of finishing its life being used to melt tar for road building. Similar locomotives, but for 760 mm gauge, had also been supplied to what later became Romanian state lines, and some of these engines still exist.

In Banská Štiavnica though, the old narrow gauge has not been forgotten but has passed into local folklore. A piece of folk theatre called the 'Salamandrovy Sprievod' takes place in the town annually in September, commemorating local history. The narrow gauge train is remembered as the 'Štiavnicka Anče' and it is now a matter of tradition that some of today's railwaymen and women take part in the theatrical display in which a large 'toy'

The old turntable at Banská Štiavnica. The pit was deeper than it at first appears, and there are some very substantial bushes growing inside! For safety's sake, and with a view to possible preservation, the turntable has been removed and transported to the Hronská Dúbrava end of the line.
Photo: Courtesy ŽSR.

The driver of the first train on the standard gauge. Photo: Courtesy ŽSR, Banská Štiavnica.

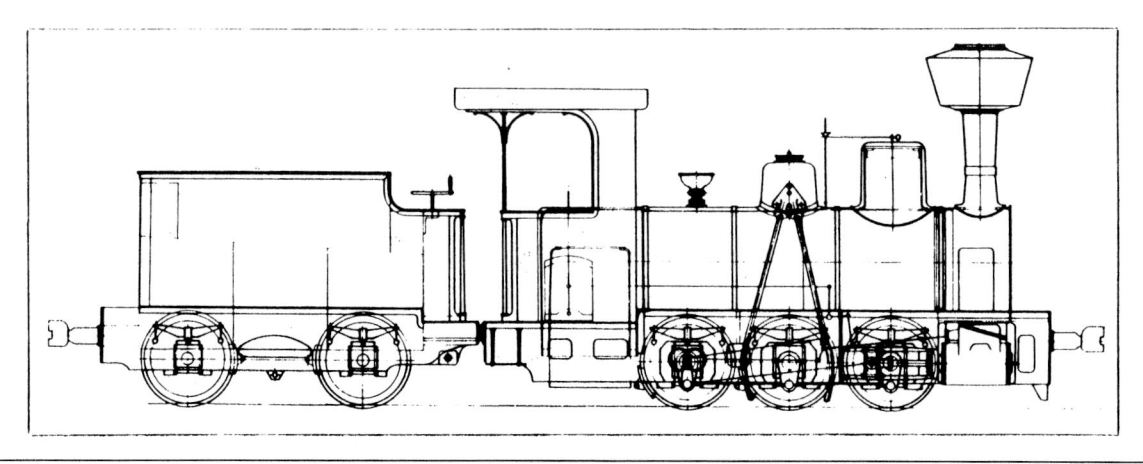

Young people working on building the "Trať Mládeže" in the summer of 1947. Photo: Courtesy ŽSR, Banská Štiavnica.

U35.104 with a mixed train at an unidentified location on the line. The photo probably dates from the period 1938-45 as the van on the right is lettered SŽ, for the Slovenskej Železnice.
Photo: Kubáček family collection.

locomotive, big enough for a man to sit in, and capable of making smoke (!) is wheeled through the streets in a parade. During the rest of the year it is kept in the mining museum with other vehicles relating to the local industry.

Margecany - Gelnica - Smolník
(Hung. Margitfalva - Golnicbanya - Szomolnok)

This was a 23 km long, metre-gauge branch built by the main Kosice - Bohumin Railway from Margecany to Gelnica, opened on 27th December 1884 and later extended 9 km on to Smolník. All along the Gelnica valley, there were old iron working, many of them dating back to the middle ages. It is believed that these old iron workings had led to some of the first primitive railways being developed, using wooden rails and wheels.

How much freight was actually carried by the new railway is unknown, for the line was equipped with only four small 0-6-0 tank locos during its whole life. These were ČSD U36.001-4, built in 1884 by Hagans.

In pre-war Czechoslovakia, the section between Margecany and Mníšek nad Hnilcom was converted to standard gauge, as part of the CSD's construction of a new central Slovak main line during the 1930s. The original locos were used in the re-gauging works during 1933-1936, and the three engines which stayed in Czechoslovakia after the War remained in use on the line between Mníšek nad Hnilcom to Smolník.

U36.004 was used on works trains during conversion of the Banská Štiavnica line, then transferred to the Čermel Pioneer Railway, where it hauled the inaugural train on 27th September 1955. The other two locos remained at work on their original line until it closed in 1966. U36.003 was later preserved and displayed at Spišská Nová Ves, but was sent to České Velenice works in 1989 and restored for operational use. It is now used on the former Pioneers' Railway in Košice, and carries the name 'Katka'.

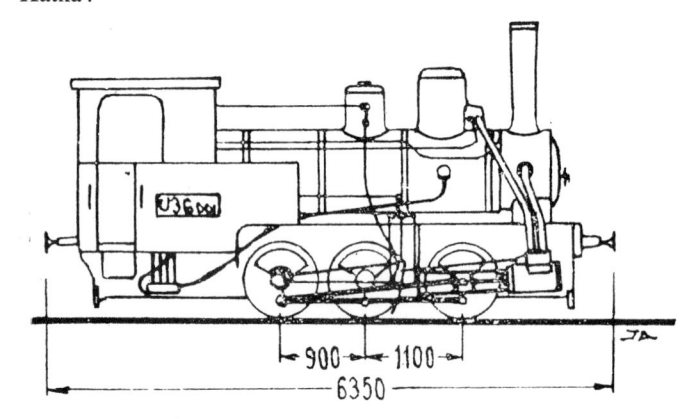

U.36.001, drawn by Josef Janata for the 'Atlas Lokomotiv'.

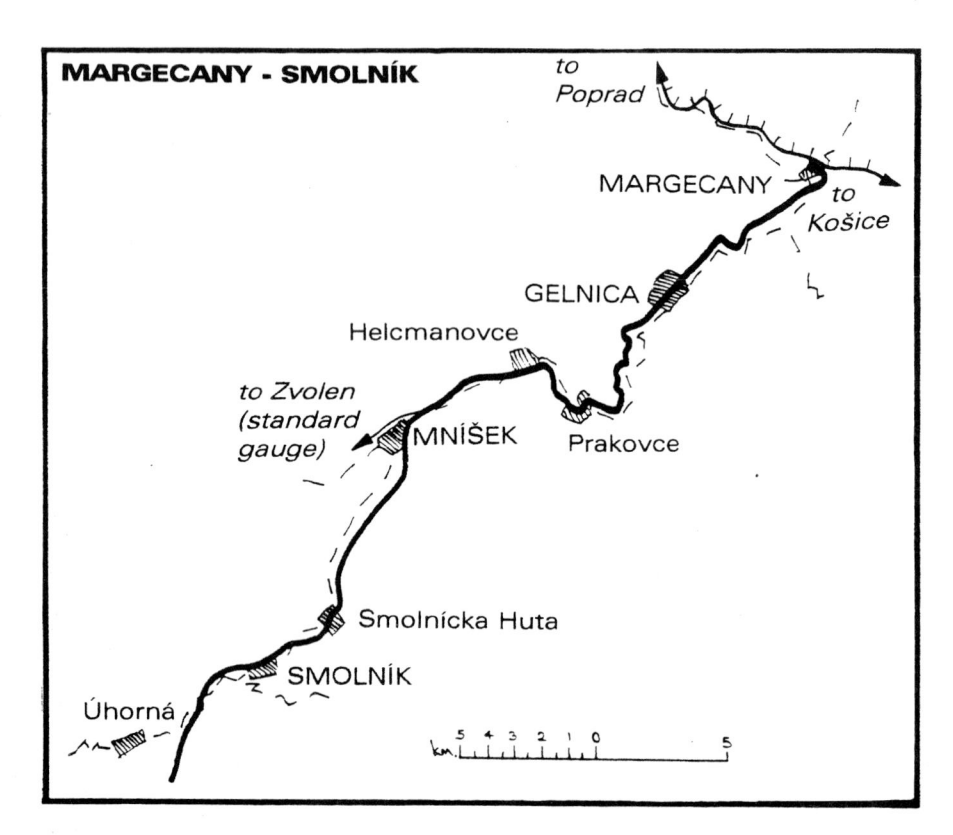

37c Mníšek nad Hnilcom — Smolnícka Huta (Úzkorozchodná železnica)

	8531 3.	8533 3.	8535 3.	8537 3.	8539 3.	km	Číslo vlaku Trieda	Rlad. Košice	Číslo vlaku Trieda	km	8532 3.	8534 3.	8536 3.	8538 3.	8540 3.
...	7.10 7.29 7.50	11.30 11.49 12.10	15.40 15.59 16.20	18.20 18.39 19.00	X 23.29 23.42 X 24.00	0 3 9	odch. Mníšek nad Hnilcom 37q ▼ Smolnická Píla z prich. Smolnícka Huta		prich. ▲ odch.	9 6 0	6.25 6.13 5.50	9.35 9.23 9.00	14.05 13.53 13.30	17.50 17.38 17.15	X 21.06 20.54 X 20.35

62

ARMOURED TRAINS IN SLOVAKIA

1. The Czechoslovakian Army's Armoured Trains 1918-39

The first armoured trains in Slovakia were built for the Austro-Hungarian armies' use in the First World War, not so much to stand as independent fighting units, but for transport of soldiers and war materials. Railways were then still the fastest means of strategic transport in rural central Europe. In 1918 some of the 'Panzerzüg' trains of the collapsing Habsburg empire fell into newly independent Czechoslovakian hands, and were put to use almost immediately.

Slovakian independence was officially declared on 30th October 1918 in Martin, two days after the Czech state was formed, and a further declaration was made in Martin on 12th November announcing a joint state of Czechs and Slovaks. Ruthenia and an area of Sub-Carpthian Russia joined Czechoslovakia on 8th May 1919.

Although the Czechs and Moravians had their parts of the country recognised without any trouble, the Slovaks and people in the far eastern areas had to defend their independence with force. The main problem was the number of Magyars who wanted the land to remain Hungarian. Many of these people were in good positions in public office, but there were also soldiers in a Hungarian Red Army seeking to establish a Communist Hungary. The result was a Hungarian uprising, to which was added the further complication of mixed ethnic groups in the Sub-Carpathian region.

Romania had also gained independence from Hungary in 1918, hence Czechoslovakian and Romanian soldiers joined forces during hostilities. The Ukrainian army units in Sub-Carpathia also came into the fray to defend Czechoslovakia in 1919. In the English-speaking countries we tend to think of the First World War in terms of the battlefields of northern France and Belgium, but Ruthenia and Galicia, although not subjected to trench warfare in the same way, were devastated by armies moving back and forth ravaging the country. Fighting continued from November 1918 until June 1919 in Slovakia, and further east it lasted even longer, finally ending with a declaration at Jasina on 23rd July 1920.

The trains put to use during the defence of Slovakia had been numbered by their former operators, and to these were added locally built 'Panzer' trains. The train sets were re-numbered by the Czechoslovakian army in the summer of 1919 after the uprising had been put down, by which time the proliferation of numbers had made for a certain amount of confusion! To try and introduce an element of clarity here the former numbers are referred to in Roman numerals and the later numbers in Arabic.

At the end of the war elements of 'Panzerzüg' nos. I, II and VI were stationed in Prague, but were despatched to Slovakia within a week of the Armistice. The first train to go was number II, consisting of ex-MÁV armoured 0-6-0T 377.116 (ČSD 310.412), two machine-gun cars 140-914 and S150-003, and heavy gun car 7-98499, to which was added machine-gun car S150-271 from Panzerzüg VII, captured on 17th November from the occupied station at Jablonice u Trnavy, en route.

The machine-gun cars were equipped with five guns (8 mm Schwarzlose M.7.12), two on each side and one at the end. The heavy gun car carried a Škoda 70 mm cannon at the front, originally from a motor torpedo boat, and a Škoda 47 mm cannon on the left side. Armour plating for the gun wagons was a sandwich of 12 mm steel outer plates, 45 mm of oak planking and 8 mm steel inner plates. Underneath was a water tank to provide an extra supply for the locomotive and extra protection. As each gun car was individually built variations did occur between the various trains.

Armoured train no.1, as it was numbered after hostilities had ended, but with only one of the machine-gun cars. In addition to their main armaments, a row of openings for rifles is visible above the roof line on both vehicles. The locomotive is ČSD 0-6-0T 310.412 'Vlasta'.
Photo: Kubáček family collection.

63

Locomotive 377.362 (ČSD 310.440) from train VI and machine-gun car S140-971 from train I were also despatched to Slovakia, enabling train II, which was a little heavy for the 0-6-0T, to be split. Both trains were in use through the spring of 1919 until 24th June 1919, when a truce was agreed. The only significant damage suffered was on 13th June at Hronské Breznice (today known as Hronská Dúbrava). The machine-gun car of one of the trains was badly damaged, though it was later repaired.

The two trains were officially numbered 1 & 2 after hostilities, and a number 3 was also gained. The Hungarians had sent their train number IV, former Austro-Hungarian number VII, to support the insurgents in Slovakia, and it became stranded at Sečovice station. Locomotive 377.455, heavy gun car 141-172 and machine-gun car S149-202 were sent to Plzeň for overhaul, and the loco was later renumbered to ČSD 310.450. Thus Czechoslovakia posessed three of the ten locomotives that the Austro-Hungarian army had armoured.

A fourth was created at Vrútky in 1919 by armouring another locomotive of the same type, ex-MÁV 377.483 (ČSD 310.453), and building a pair of gun wagons on flat-wagon chassis. A captured Italian large-bore gun was used for the heavy gun car. The train formed actually became number VII, as there were other trains built, and numbering did not follow in sequence.

The Královopolsko steelworks in Brno created some of the armoured trains, including one named 'Brno' with loco 478.12, which was used in northern Moravia securing the Polish border and did not work in Slovakia. Two other trains were assembled in Brno, train III 'Bratislava' and train IV 'Generál Štefánik'.

The armament of 'Bratislava' consisted of a 75 mm M.15 cannon and two Maxim machine guns mounted in cars 168.660 and 171.130. The train was despatched to Slovakia on 18th June 1919, but came to grief two days later at Nové Zámky when the forward part of the train plunged off a small bridge destroyed by the Hungarians. In the August it arrived at Škoda, Plzeň for repair, but it was not deemed worth the work, so the re-usable parts were de-armoured and returned to normal railway service. The vacant number was used for the train already mentioned whch was then being built at Plzeň.

The third train from Brno, number IV, reached Bratislava on 3rd July 1919. A non-armoured locomotive was used, no. 66.01 (ČSD class 314.3, ex-Kaiser Ferdinands Nordbahn), but was later replaced by armoured 2-8-0T 179.01 (ČSD 421.001). The train itself consisted of a wagon with cannons at either end and two machine-gun cars. In company with train I, it was deployed at Lučenec and remained there until 1923, when both trains were retired to Milovice, not far from Nymburk. Another of the ex-StEG class 40s was armoured, number 179.05 (ČSD 421.05) and may have served with train V, which was also in other respects identical to train IV.

Some swapping of locos between trains occurred in 1920 as 377.483 from train VII was loaned to train III while 377.455 was having an overhaul, and then joined train IV, and so ended up going to Milovice when that train was withdrawn. Train VII at this time also needed repairs and in 1921 was also withdrawn.

During the first half of 1919 a further train was built at Škoda, Plzeň, consisting of a class 377 loco, two heavy gun cars, each equipped with a 75 mm cannon and machine-guns. Car numbers were 316.603 and 333.509, and confusingly this was train 2, though it does not seem to conform to the post-hostility train number 2. In Slovakia it was strengthened with parts of train VII, and a further improvised car on which was mounted an 80 mm field gun, making it the most formidable armoured train of the period. In this form the consist was based in the south of Slovakia.

A pair of trains, numbers 5 'Plzeň' and 6 'Praha' were built at Škoda in the spring of 1919, and utilised two class 99 2-6-0s for each train. These were 99.12/13/16 (ČSD 320.008/009/012) from the Karlovy Vary - Mariánské Lázně branch, and 99.67 (ČSD 320.032) from the Karlovy Vary - Merklin line. These four locos were protected by armour plating from 3.25 to 6 mm thick according to which part of the loco it was protecting.

The trains as a whole were designed symmetrically to be able to operate effectively in both directions, so the locomotives were sandwiched between two machine-gun cars, outside which were the two heavy gun cars. These each carried a pair of turrets equipped with a 70 mm cannon and a machine-gun, between which was a short observation tower. The machine-gun cars had five guns on each side, with additional openings for rifles, and two pairs of rifle openings on the roof. There was also a more substantial hatch in the roof to allow the use of machine guns for protection against aerial attack or firing of mortars. Between the axles was a 4.5m^2 water tank and room for an extra half tonne of coal for the engines.

Trains 5 and 6 arrived too late to take part in any action, but remained in Slovakia until the autumn of 1923, by which time the situation had settled down and all the trains were put into store at Milovice. The idea was to overhaul and upgrade the trains, but the ČSD had decided to charge the army for the hire of their locomotives and rolling stock from 1st January 1922. The bulk of the cost was the daily charge for each locomotive of up to Kč 234, depending on the type, and the first year of rent cost the army Kč 651,346. The next year it was even more, so in 1925 the four class 320.0 2-6-0s were de-armoured at Nymburk and returned to Karlovy Vary. The de-commissioning was undertaken in such a way that they could be re-armoured within 48 hours.

By September 1925 the remaining rolling stock had been formed into six trains whose formation remained static until March 1939, although with various items of equipment added or upgraded from time to time. The army purchased the trains from the ČSD, along with various coaches that had been used for support troops.

They also purchased an armoured draisine with a machine gun turret, built by Tatra's Koprivnice works in 1936. It carried number D2.001, and was probably the first of a standard series, as a photo exists of three together at an unknown location, possibly in Poland. The top speed was a mere 45 kph, or about 28 mph, but the service range was an astounding 435 miles. Somehow five crew members were shoe-horned into this angular bathtub on wheels.

There was a Škoda project in the 1930s to build more substantial diesel armoured railcars, but it got no further than a wooden mock-up, and by the time the Sudeten and Olsa regions were annexed there was nothing modern on rails in the country's defence force.

In late 1938 some of the trains were despatched from Milovice, but were all returned within a few months. An exception was the armoured draisine which collided with a shunter at Zvolen on 22nd November, injuring three of the crew members. Evidently it was repaired because it ended up in the Polish armoured fleet after the war. The German army took the armoured rolling stock at Milovice, but put the locomotives back into normal service, probably because the class 310.4 was rather small for use on the more substantial armoured trains of the German Army and was non-standard to the D.R.

2. The Slovak National Partisan Trains of 1944

The first of the armoured trains built by the partisans of the Slovenské národné povstanie, named 'Štefánik'. The photo was taken shortly after the train had been built, before mottled camouflage was exchanged for drab green. In addition to the armoured vehicles two support wagons are coupled to the rear of the train. Photo: Kubáček family collection.

Slovakia in the Second World War was run by a government under the thumb of Hungary, which in turn was allied to the Axis powers, indeed Hungary had moved its border northwards taking back a substantial part of Slovak territory lost when Czechoslovakia was constituted. Although nominally not invaded by Germany, the government was nevertheless basically fascist.

Local groups of activists were formed in various parts of Slovakia, ranging from saboteurs who went on raids in Hungary and Poland to clandestine presses printing propaganda. One of these produced a newspaper called 'Hlas' which was duplicated in the works at Zvolen. On 1st May 1943 some hot-headed Communist activists pushed a locomotive into the turntable well at Zvolen shed, sparking off a brutal investigation of about thirty railway workers, inspiring strong partisan feelings. In the same year railway workers from Zvolen were in contact with some soldiers from Martin who were destined for the Eastern Front, but chose the much more desirable option of defecting to the partisan movement.

Zvolen was in the right position for developments. It had the railway installations, especially the works, it was near the strongly partisan area of Banská Bystrice, and it was within easy reach of mountainous areas. The lines in the region had plenty of tunnels where partisan trains could be hidden, and of course to

65

Standing as monument to the S.N.P. below Zvolen Castle is a replica armoured train used for filming the story of the partisans. Most of the original locomotives and armoured vehicles had been long gone by then, although one armoured wagon is preserved at Banská Bystrica. The locomotive under the dummy armour is actually a post-war class 433.0 2-8-2T, a replacement for 431.014 which was used for filming, and which has recently been restored to operating condition at Vrútky. Photo: Paul Catchpole.

catch partisans in such country would be difficult.

Zvolen's partisan railwaymen gained posts in the Zvolen branch of the national Milicia, a security force, and established a railway branch responsible for policing track and installations in the district. At the same time, with the withdrawals from lost battles, large quantities of German trains and war materials were rolling back into and through Slovakia. They came under the authority of a railway commissioner and an army transport commander both of whom were Slovaks.

The main partisan movement, the Slovenské národné povstanie (S.N.P) established a group amonst the railwaymen in Zvolen works. One of the workshops at Zvolen was used to repair damaged rolling stock and railcars, and so lent itself ideally for the armouring of wagons. This workshop already had a group of partisans in the Communist Party of Slovakia, (the KSS), and they were joined by some of the Milicia infiltrators to work on the armoured trains. As work got under way others came to help.

Work started in earnest on 4th September 1944 and the first of three trains was ready in 14 days. The other two were assembled within just three more weeks. The three trains were all named after well-known national figures, "Generál M.R. Štefánik", "J.M. Hurban", and "T.G. Masaryk".

All three were built to a similar concept, but as materials and weapons were collected and improvised from various sources each vehicle was an individual. The formation was anti-mine wagon, light gun car, tank car, loco, tank car, machine-gun car. There were also support cars, which would normally be left at some nearby safe location with a non-armoured locomotive before the train went into action. Three coaches were necessary for accommodation, catering and first aid (with medical staff), plus an ammunition wagon.

The little class 310.4 0-6-0Ts were not sufficiently powerful to manage such trains, especially on local routes with stiff inclines, so three class 320.2 2-6-2Ts were used. These were ex-MÁV class 376 inherited upon formation of Czechoslovakia, ČSD numbers 320.213/216/220. The first, 320.213 received plating to the cab, boiler, dome, and over the wheels, cylinders and motion, to much the same design as the replica at Zvolen. No plating was put over 320.213's smokebox, but the other two did have this improvement, in fact 320.220's armour plating enclosed the chimney and the front of the locomotive. As the

66

locos had no tender it was decided that they would have to carry black coal as that would go further than the more readily available, but poorer quality brown coal.

The leading anti-mine wagons were pushed coupled by a long pole for safety and use was made of them for carrying a supply of track repair and re-railing materials and equipment, including 15 and 20 metre sections of rail.

The leading gun wagons were built on type U coal wagons with a brake cabin. The cabin doubled up as the entrance to the wagon and they were equipped with a low-profile conning tower and a periscope, particularly important as these cars served as the command centre for the train. The ring of the conning tower top provided a machine-gun mounting, but the main armament was an 80 mm field gun mounted at the front of the vehicle. All the wagons carrying personnel had escape hatches in the floor.

The rear gun wagons were of very similar construction, but equipped for heavy machine guns instead of a cannon. One of these was mounted at the rear of the wagon to protect the train from behind. A similar conning tower was fitted, so the train could be commanded from either end.

Tank wagons were built by mounting a type 35 light tank on a goods wagon and building 20-40 mm of armour plating around it. The turrets did not receive any extra plating at first, but this was added after a battle near Čremošné. No account is to hand as to how they 'found' spare tanks in the first place! The brake platforms of the tank wagons were left open, and the one behind the loco was coupled so that the platform was next to the bunker and could carry some extra coal.

For the first two trains the armour plating was built up from boiler plates 12 mm thick, but contact had been made with another group of partisans at the Podbrezova steelworks, so for the third train 15 mm plates were obtained for the vehicle walls and roof, 10 mm for the floors and 20 mm for the locomotive cab and brake cabins. The overall livery of the trains was green, brown and white camouflage, but it was found that the white stood out too clearly from the air, and a drab green was quickly adopted.

All three trains were tried out on the Zvolen - Krupina line before being handed over to the fighting units formed of rebel partisan soldiers, 'Štefánik' on 20th September, 'Hurban' on 29th September and Masaryk on 13th October.

Train 1, 'Štefánik was sent south-west of Zvolen to work between Hronská Dübrava and Kremnice and was engaged in a battle against the SS at Svätý Kríž nad Hronom on 4th October. After a return to Zvolen the train was relocated to the Zvolen - Krupina line, but was called south to trouble around Dobrá Niva from 19th to 22nd October. It took part in a counter attack and some of the crew were lost under fire from aircraft. After a few days on the Zvolen - Kriváň line 'Štefánik' went on 25th October via Zvolen and Banská Bystrice to Ul'anka, it's last tour of duty.

'Hurban' was sent out for service around Banská Bystrica and Malý Šturec, but with fighting to the north-west it was despatched on 4th October up the line up towards Diviaky. Near Čremošné station both the armoured train and the support train came under attack that day. The two tank wagons were badly damaged with the loss of partisan soldiers' lives, so the trains returned to Zvolen for repairs and strengthening. Afterwards 'Hurban' was despatched back to the area and remained there supporting the partisans until 27th October.

The third train, 'Masaryk' was sent up to the upper Hron region between Brezno nad Hronom and Červená Skála, to further back up partisan action. Some damage was sustained on 21st October, but repairs were quickly carried out and it was back in action very quickly. 'Hurban' was sent up to Červená Skála in the mean time and supported a successful counter attack, ending up at Brezno nad Hronom.

On 24th October, however, at Pohorelskej Maši 320.220 on the 'Masaryk' train was destroyed with the loss of the crew. There was no time for any repairs due to progress of the fascist forces and a non-armoured locomotive was hurriedly despatched to bring the train back to the Banská Bystrica - Diviaky line where it was left in one of the many tunnels. 'Hurban' also returned to this line and finished it's time at Horný Harmanec, today known as Harmanec Jaskyňa.

The S.N.P. armoured trains were not active for very long, but provided valuable support to the partisan army prior to the liberation of Czechoslovakia by the Soviet Red Army.

Working on the Railways

A 1939-45 Slovenské Železnice track maintenance gang take a break at an unknown location. The locomotive is 310.512, an 0-6-0T of Hungarian origin.
Photo: Courtesy ŽSR.

A larger gang at work on track construction or repair, also in the SŽ period, as shown by the markings on the wagons. Pracovný vozeň means working vehicle.
Photo: Courtesy ŽSR.

68

The locomotive is a class 333.1, judging from the curve over the middle driving wheel, and it is carrying a ČSD number plate, so the photo was taken after 1925, but as to the identity of the people and location there is no clue. Photo: Kubáček family collection.

A woman's work is never done! The ladies cleaning team at Zvolen depot is bringing a special shine to rebuilt ex-KBD 2-6-2 no. 365.315. The date unknown. Photo: Courtesy ŽSR.

69

One of the less pleasant tasks at a steam locomotive running shed is the dusty, dirty work of cleaning out the smokebox at the end of a turn. The location is Vrútky, and the loco is 365.428, an ex-DR class 64 2-6-2T, which places the photo post-1945. If anybody deserved a Socialist era peoples' hero medal it's working men doing a job like these two.
Photo: Courtesy ŽSR.

Boiler repairs the hard way. The man with the big hammer strikes the chisel to shear off a rivet, then the third man removes the stub.
Photo: Courtesy ŽSR.

Left: Preparing a freight for despatch from Trenčianska Teplá in February 1998. One man taps wheels, and checks the brakes and couplings, while the other with the cap tickets up each wagon.

Above: The wheel-tapper. Leopoldov, October 1997.

Below: A lengthman walks through Kral'ovany with a can of paint and a long brush, preparing for the maintenance crew.

Photos on this page: Paul Catchpole.

'Dovidenia'